HOME IS EVERYWHERE

HOME IS EVERYWHERE

The Unbelievably True Story of One Man's
Journey to Map America

CHARLES L. NOVAK

DISRUPTION
BOOKS

Austin   New York

This book is memoir. It reflects the author's present recollections of experiences over time. Some names and characteristics have been changed, some events have been compressed, and some dialogue has been recreated.

Published by Disruption Books
Austin, TX, and New York, NY
www.disruptionbooks.com

Distributed by Disruption Books

For ordering information or special discounts for bulk purchases, please contact Disruption Books at info@disruptionbooks.com.

Cover design, text design, and composition by Kim Lance.

Print ISBN: 978-1-63331-032-2
eBook ISBN: 978-1-63331-033-9

First Edition

To my wonderful family.

Contents

Foreword

THIS IS A BOOK ABOUT THE greatest man I've ever known.

If you come from a humble background, this book will give you hope. If you come from a life of privilege, it will help you never take what you have for granted. If you want a look at how vastly this nation has changed over the course of one man's lifetime, you'll find that in these pages, too.

As the cofounder, chairman, and CEO of Yum! Brands—the owner of Pizza Hut, Taco Bell, and KFC—I've had the good fortune to meet world leaders, international celebrities, and countless phenomenal people over the course of my lifetime. But for me, the man who stands head and shoulders above the lot is my father, Charles Novak. He's an authentic man with uncanny common sense and a wicked sense of humor, and he comes from Haddam, Kansas, a little farming town that you've probably never heard of.

You'll see in these pages that my father has had an amazing life: crisscrossing America, living in trailers and tents, in small towns and out-of-the-way locales, all across this great nation. He lived this unconventional life because of his job as a surveyor mapping America for the federal government. He married my mom Jean, and she joined him and the other families on his survey party, traveling with him from place to place. When they had my two sisters, Susan and Karen, and me, we came along for the ride. All in all, Dad has lived in more than sixty small towns in more than twenty states over the course of his career. I don't know anyone else who has lived a life like that.

So what can be learned from a life like his? Well, just about everything that matters most. You'll learn that hard work, an adventurous spirit, and a can-do attitude can take you pretty far in this life, even if you come from the humblest of beginnings. You'll see just how far one man can travel, both literally and figuratively. To think that when Dad was born, you couldn't even locate many of this country's small towns on a map, and now—thanks to the work of my dad and people like him—any one of us can navigate ourselves to just about any location in the fifty states with the help of GPS . . . well, that's a pretty amazing thing to contemplate.

It wasn't always an easy life, but Dad has never been one to complain. He and my mom were always clear about their main goal in life: to give their kids a chance to live the American Dream. My sisters and I are proof that my parents more than succeeded. Yet as I read the details of his life— including some stories I've never heard before—something occurred to me: My dad lived the American Dream as well. And given where he started out, his was the biggest achievement of all.

Most of all, I've learned from my parents that home is something you can create for yourself, wherever you are and whatever your circumstances. All you need is the right intention and the company of people you love. I still remember the five of us—my parents, my sisters, and me—spending evenings together in our trailer in Dodge City or someplace like it. Because we were packed in such a small space, we'd always end up clumped together on the couch, watching programs on television like *The Ed Sullivan Show*. No matter how big our homes have gotten since then, or how much our families have grown, when we're together these days, we still find ourselves all clumped together like that—because for us, that's what home is all about. That's why, as long as we're together, home can be anywhere and everywhere.

For these reasons and more, I believe that everyone should read this book (and I'm not just saying that because my dad wrote it). Plus, Dad's a heck of a storyteller, so I have no doubt you'll enjoy this story of the greatest man I've ever known.

David Novak

Introduction

I BEGAN WRITING THIS BOOK IN 2017, the year I turned eighty-eight years old. It starts where many personal histories start: at the time when I was born, which in my case happened in the spring of 1929, just a few months before America was hit by the Great Depression. The place was Haddam, Kansas, a small town with a population of just 381 people, according to the 1930 U.S. Census. All in all, I had a pretty modest start. I don't think anyone could have predicted the kind of life I'd live or where I'd end up.

Over the course of my nearly ninety years, I've lived in more than sixty places across this great nation, including twice in Dodge City, Kansas, and in Alaska three times. I have lived everywhere from Crookston, Minnesota, in the north to Raymondville, Texas, in the south; from Gorham, New Hampshire, in the east to Crescent, Oregon, in the west. And in a whole lot of towns in between.

Who lives this nomadic kind of life? Someone who ends up in my line of work. By luck, or maybe by accident, I landed a job as a surveyor for a federal agency called the U.S. Coast and Geodetic Survey. That agency was responsible for creating and managing a national system of geodetic controls, which was the basis for creating maps of cities and counties across the United States, charting our nation's waters, enabling communications, along with numerous other crucial applications. Many years later, when GPS technology was invented, it was our system that was used to test GPS satellites for accuracy and to readjust the geodetic controls in the national network.

In order to create and maintain this system, groups of us traveled the country for many years. We lived mostly in trailers, though sometimes we stayed in motels, rented rooms, or even tents pitched in far-flung places. When I got married, and later when I had children, my family traveled with me. It was a life I never could have dreamed of while growing up in a small farming community in northern Kansas.

In fact, *I never could have dreamed of this* became something of a theme as I watched the world change, living through several wars, the civil rights era, and some amazing developments in technology. When I was growing up in Haddam, we didn't even have an indoor shower, and we went to the outhouse to use the bathroom. Now I live in a big, beautiful home with air-conditioning, cable television, and more than one computer. It's nearly impossible to state how far I've come and how much things have changed.

The life I live today is something I never could have conceived of for myself or for anyone else. All I knew at the age of eighteen, when I was getting ready to leave Haddam, was that I wanted to have a good life—and that I was willing to work hard, adapt, and do whatever I needed to do to get it. That drive plus a little good luck were enough to take me to some pretty great places and open up the way to some extraordinary things. I've seen a lot, probably more than most people. As I've traveled all over the United States, I've met some interesting people, climbed a few mountains, and gotten myself out of more than one tricky (sometimes even danger-ous) situation. I met a wonderful girl—my wife, Jean—and we raised three remarkable kids, all of whom attended college (something neither of us ever did) and lead highly successful lives. And I had a pretty good time along the way, too.

This is that story, and this seems to be the right moment to tell it. We're living in a time when a lot of people in this country are unhappy about a lot of different things, and maybe some of them have a point. But I often think that if they had started off their lives like I did—if they had seen and experienced as much change in their own circumstances and in the world around them as I have—they might be a little more optimistic about how things will turn out.

Looking back over the life I've led, one that I never could have ever thought possible, even I am not entirely sure how I managed to get here. What I do know is that it's been quite a journey—one that I wouldn't trade for anything.

A Short History of Haddam, Kansas
39° 51' 23" N, 97° 18' 10" W

THE TOWN OF HADDAM, LOCATED IN Washington County, Kansas, about ten miles south of the Nebraska border, was founded in 1869. It was named after another town of Haddam, located in Connecticut.

The first store in Haddam was opened by J. W. Taylor that same year, and steady growth followed. At one point, more than forty businesses were active in the town. West Haddam was established around the same time, and the two towns were rivals until they merged in 1874.

An all-woman city council, mayor, clerk, and police judge were elected in 1901, at a time when women still didn't have the right to vote. These women were defeated in an election the following year, but during their short time in office, they oversaw the building of a stone jail for the grand sum of $325. That jail still stands just off Main Street next to a sign that reads: "Built for the confinement of Haddam's unruly men."

What's now called Main Street—the main artery through town—used to be part of the old U.S. Highway 36. When that highway moved three miles south of town in the early 1940s, it was a disaster for Haddam and other small towns on the old route.

The 1940 U.S. Census recorded the population in Haddam as 384. As of the 2010 Census, the population had dropped to 104.

Haddam, Kansas, U.S.A.

FOR MY BIRTHDAY ONE YEAR NOT long ago, someone gave me a book that tells about the many notable events that happened during the year I was born. It was 1929, the year that Babe Ruth became the first professional baseball player to hit five hundred career home runs. 7Up was invented that year, and the very first Academy Awards were presented by the Academy of Motion Picture Arts and Sciences. (Best Picture went to the silent film *Wings*, if you can remember that one.) It was a transitional year in politics, with Calvin Coolidge holding the office of United States president until March 4, followed by Herbert Hoover for his first and only term. It was also a year of advancements in business and technology, including the patenting of the first gasoline-powered chain saw, the introduction of frozen foods (thanks to a new quick-freezing process developed by Clarence Birdseye), and the historic completion of a round-the-world flight by the passenger-carrying German airship, *Graf Zeppelin*. Most famously, 1929 was the year the stock market crashed—on October 24, known as Black Tuesday—kicking off the Great Depression.

Somewhat less famously, on May 25 of that year—five months before Black Tuesday—I was born in the town of Haddam, Kansas. Haddam was just a small farming community then, and there wasn't much else going. If you didn't farm, you worked at a grocery store, a gas station, or one of the other businesses in town, because that's all there was to do. The town of Haddam was essentially one street: Main Street, where you could find just about everything the town had to offer. It was part of U.S. Highway 36, which was a gravel road at the time. All the other roads, off the main highway, were dirt.

When I was young, Main Street was a busy place. It started with City Hall on the north end, followed by just about anything you could ask for in those days. Haddam had a restaurant, a pool hall, two garages, a hotel, and a motel catering to the people that the highway brought through town. We had two gas stations, two barbershops, two creameries, a blacksmith, a butcher shop, and a lumberyard. Then there were the stores—the grocery store, the general store, the hardware store, and the drug store—as well as the usual places, like the post office, the bank, and the telephone company. There was even a hatchery, where eggs gave way to baby chicks, and our very own newspaper, the *Haddam Gazette*, which had an office with a printing press. The paper published local and county news. Practically anyone could write an article, and the *Gazette* would print it.

One of the businesses along Main Street was a Ford garage owned by a guy named W. T. Rooney. When people came into town who didn't know him, he would bet them a dollar that he could stare at the sun for five minutes. He always won. Of course, it was a surefire bet: Mr. Rooney had a glass eye, but you couldn't tell. He'd close his good eye and look at the sun with his glass one, never letting on that he was fudging. That old guy was one of the real characters in town.

At the end of the street was an open area where an outdoor movie theater was set up on Wednesday nights. Local business owners sponsored the movies to encourage people to come into town. It was started by a guy named Edward Wransky, who would always show westerns like *Hop-Along Cassidy*. (Not much else was available back then.) The screen would be set up on a couple of wooden planks, and a projector was brought in on the back of a small trailer. After World War II, Mr. Wransky took this show on the road, hiring guys who had come out of the army to pull the trailer from town to town and show the movies. He'd schedule their trips and pay them five dollars per trip. That's all they got, even though they had to travel around in their own car. Each town got its own night of the week. It was a good idea, and Mr. Wransky made lots of money off his little investment.

Just behind Main Street, on the northeast side, was a small hospital with a cemetery. Railroad tracks ran behind the south side of the street, with a grain elevator and a railroad depot set alongside them. The little stone jail (which got pretty good use, as I recall) was back there behind the bank, where it remains today.

And that was basically it. Everything you could need, really. That was the main town of Haddam.

Off the main road, there were mostly just homes and farms. There was a Methodist church and an evangelist congregation, one of those filled with holy rollers. And we had our own high school on the top of the hill, as well as a grade school in the lower part of town. I was one of just seventeen kids in my high school class. There were even fewer in my grade school, because some kids went to country schools at that age.

I remember in grade school, if you didn't toe the mark, you went to the cloakroom and got the strap. One trip to the cloakroom, and you didn't want a second one. That's how teachers made sure kids behaved. I never got sent to the cloakroom myself, but I certainly heard stories from the ones who did. Teachers can't do that today, but back in those days, that's what happened. A lot of things were different back then—some things for better, and some for worse.

A grade school photo from Haddam, Kansas

☀

I lived in Haddam from the time I was born, in 1929, to 1947, when I graduated from high school—a period of time that included the Great Depression, World War II, and Prohibition, which lasted a lot longer in Kansas than anywhere else in the country. My dad was a farmer when I was born. When he and my mom got married, his parents had given them eighty acres of land. That wasn't much land to make a living off of, and they lost it during the Depression.

In fact, all five kids in my dad's family got the same wedding present, and only one was able to hold on to his farm during the Depression. That was Uncle Joe, and he had to get a second job to do it. He traveled all around Kansas, refereeing basketball games. He made enough money that way to save his farm.

Basketball was always big in my family. One time, I went along with Uncle Joe to a game that he was refereeing somewhere in southern Kansas. He had this 1936 Ford with gas heaters inside the car on the floor of the passenger side. It was wintertime, and I was sitting there with a pretty good pair of dress shoes on. I fell asleep with my shoes on that heater, and it just melted the wax right off them. I didn't even wake up. You didn't want to get too close to those gas heaters.

After losing the farm, my family moved about five miles away, into town, to a house just off Main Street. I don't really remember the farm, because I was so young when we left it. I do remember that my dad was gone a lot when I was growing up. After the farm, he got a job as an engineer on the railroad, working out of Lincoln, Nebraska.

My mother didn't want to move to Lincoln. She had grown up in Haddam, and her whole family was there. She didn't want to take us kids to Nebraska, either. So we stayed in Haddam, and Dad lived in Lincoln a lot of the time. Lincoln was about one hundred miles away, so he could only come back when he wasn't working.

Dad's name was Emil Charles Novak. His parents came to America from the Czechoslovak region where Novak is a pretty common last name. They spoke Czech when my dad was growing up, and he could speak it too. I never learned, because my mother didn't know the language, and Dad only spoke it when he was around his siblings or the few other Czechs in town. His parents died when they were in their fifties, so I never knew them at all. Today that may seem young, but passing away at that age wasn't all that uncommon back then: the average lifespan was only fifty-something years old.

Dad was a baseball player when he was young—a catcher and a third baseman. He and his three brothers were all really good ball players. They used to go to places like Denver to play in tournaments. When he was about eighteen years old, my dad went to the Yankees farm club out in Twin Falls, Idaho. He'd never been away from home before that, not for a long period of time anyway. He went out there, and he didn't last. He got into it with the manager, and the next thing he knew, he was back in Haddam. I think that was the way he wanted it. He got homesick, being so far away. But he kept playing baseball with guys in town until he was fifty years old. Even at that age, he could still catch pretty well.

When my dad was around, he always wanted me to wear a hat whenever I left the house. He always wore a hat himself, so I guess that's what he thought men should do. But I never wanted to wear it. I would put it on, and then once I got out the door, I would stash it someplace. Then I would pick it up before I came back home, and he'd never know the difference.

When I was young, I had some pretty strong opinions about what I wanted to wear. For example, I hated blue jeans. I'd only wear khakis to school if I could help it. I don't know why. For some reason, I just didn't want anything to do with blue jeans.

My mother's name was Lula Retha. She spent her days taking care of the home and us kids. One of her specialties was making pancakes in the mornings, with homemade sugar syrup. Another one of her talents was chicken and noodles. Everybody—all my aunts and uncles—wanted to come to our place to eat Mom's chicken and noodles. Her noodles were homemade, rolled out flat, and then cut to size. She'd have them laying all over the house, because she had all us kids plus the aunts and uncles to feed. That's a lot of noodles.

After making the noodles, she would take the chicken and boil it for the broth. I like a lot of broth on my noodles, because that's the way she made it. We'd have it with mashed potatoes. Oh, it was really good.

I have three brothers and three sisters—seven of us in all. My sister Donna is the oldest. I was the second born in the family. Then came my sister Ila Lee and my brothers, James, Verlin, and Danny Joe. Finally there was Peggy, the youngest. As far as I can remember, all of us were born at home, delivered by Dr. Wall. That was pretty normal in those days.

When my youngest sister Peggy was on the way, my mother sent us off to school early so she could have her. I remember thinking to myself as I walked to school, *The last thing we need is another sister*. It seemed to me that there were enough of us already.

Our house in town wasn't too big, but it wasn't too small either. It had a living room, a dining area, a kitchen, and one bedroom for my parents on the first floor. When I was young, there wasn't a sewer system, so we had outdoor toilets and we heated up buckets of water on the stove when we wanted to take a tub bath. That was a lot of trouble, though, so if I could help it, I would shower at school. Then, when I was in seventh or eighth grade, we finally had a bathroom put in downstairs.

The upstairs was divided in two—boys on one side, and girls on the other. My brothers and I had our side set up as a wide-open space with just beds in there. It was close, but we all got along pretty well. We didn't spend that much time together in our room anyway, unless we were sleeping. When the weather was right, we would get outside. The house had no air-conditioning, so in the summertime, we'd even take a blanket and go outside to sleep. It was cooler to lie on the ground.

It got so hot in Haddam in the summer. Back then, the houses weren't insulated too well. They didn't use drywall like they do now. Instead, they had plaster and plasterboard for siding.

It got cold in Haddam, too, in the wintertime. When we got a good snow, everything would just shut down. The whole town was quiet. At the time, the country roads were lined with hedgerows. That paralyzed everything, because the snow would get packed in there, boxed in by the hedges. To clear it, a Caterpillar would be brought in to buck that snow for a long time. So people would just get stuck wherever they were until the road opened again.

⁂

In the mid-1930s, the Great Drought—what was called "the Dust Bowl"—made the Depression even worse, especially in farming communities like Haddam. I was still young, but I remember things being pretty tough for everybody. What I remember most is the effect it had on my grandparents' farm, where I used to spend the summer months as a child.

This was my mother's side of the family. Her dad—his name was Frank—was from a German background, and he came from upstate New York. My grandmother, Mattie, was of Dutch ancestry, from a strong Quaker family, and she was a very neat lady, always dressed nice with her hair combed straight back and tied in a tidy bun. Both came from farming families that moved out west to Kansas because they got land grants from the government to start farms. That's the story I heard, anyway.

During the drought, these huge cracks appeared in the earth on my grandparents' farm reaching clear across the fields. It was kind of a scary thing for a kid, because the cracks were at least six inches wide, and they looked bottomless. I thought if I fell into one of the cracks, there would be nowhere to land.

Then there was the time the grasshoppers took over. You could look up into the sky, and it was just black with them, like these huge, dark clouds hanging there—only the clouds were swarms of grasshoppers. Farmers would plow a furrow around their crops, hoping the grasshoppers would land on the bare ground rather than the fields. Otherwise, they would eat everything in sight.

This one time, there were just too many grasshoppers—enough to clean out an entire farm. They came through, and by the time they left, the crops were gone. The grasshoppers wouldn't bother people. They would just go wherever they found something green to eat, which became harder and harder as the drought dragged on.

When a young kid sees stuff like this, it really makes an impression. But despite these few scary memories, I really liked spending time at the farm and with my grandparents.

My granddad was one to go out and have a beer every once in a while, and he would often take me with him. On Saturdays, he would take produce from the farm into town to sell, and then he would sit and have his couple of beers and a rare hamburger with raw onions on a bun. (Those old-timers, they ate a lot of undercooked meat.) I would sit with my granddad, and he'd tell me stories about life before he got married. He had this horse and buggy that he would take out to go "courting," as he called it—mostly to dances, which were held in a nearby town, about eight miles away. By the time I was a kid, he had a 1929 or 1930 REO touring car—a big, black, four-door car. One Saturday, he drove it to town and burnt out the motor going home. I think he'd had too much to drink. That was the last car he owned.

My granddad's first wife passed away during childbirth, so then he married her sister. He had one son and four daughters with his first wife, and then three more kids with the second. My mother was the middle child— and the favorite, I'm sure—of the second wife.

In addition to Saturdays, every Wednesday my grandparents would go to town to see a movie and purchase supplies. My grandmother would always drop by on the way to visit my mother and me. Just like my mother was her favorite, I'm also sure I was her favorite grandchild. My grandmother liked Milky Way candy bars—they were the big thing back then, along with Baby Ruths—and that was one thing I could always look forward to. When she came to visit, she would always say to me, "Charles, let's sit down at the table and share this candy bar." At that time, Milky Ways were huge—three times the size you get now—and you could buy one for five cents.

Because I was her favorite, my grandmother would always want to take me home with her to the farm, and I was always happy to go there, particularly to eat. She and my granddad grew just about anything you could want: wheat, corn, alfalfa, an acre of potatoes. I picked potatoes until I was just about green in the face. They had no basement, but an opening underneath the house led to a big storage bin where they put the potatoes, which would last all winter long.

They also had game and other animals at the farm. My Aunt Hazel—I was always her favorite, too—used to say, "Charles, go out and catch a chicken for lunch." She would get the hot water ready, and I would go outside and put out a line of grain to lure the chickens. Then I'd grab one. It was easy. My aunt would wring the chicken's neck and dump it in the hot water to take the feathers off. Then she'd cut it up and fry it, and we'd have fried chicken for lunch. It tasted amazing, as fresh as you can imagine.

From time to time, my grandparents would butcher a pig out on the farm and bring half of it to my family. First they would fry down the pork and put it in a five-gallon crock. Then they would take the fat from frying the pork and pour it over the meat to preserve it. That way, anytime you wanted pork for dinner, you would just get some out of the crock and heat it up. It was already cooked, and it was so good. One time, while I was staying with my grandparents, they hired my older cousin Bill as a farmhand. My granddad had a set of mules, named Molly and Jack, and a set of horses, one of which pulled the buggy around. I liked to go out into the fields when someone was working with the animals, so I was out there one day when

Bill was walking behind Jack the mule and got kicked in the head. I was just a little kid at the time, and it really frightened me—my cousin, just lying there on the dirt, out cold. So I went running back to the house to tell my grandmother, "Jack kicked Bill in the head, and he's dead!"

My grandparents took off toward the fields, but by the time they got to Bill, he was already standing up. I had never seen anything like it before. I was just a young fella, so to me it was like he had risen from the dead.

At that age, I thought farmwork was fun. Once I was old enough to do a lot of the hard labor, I changed my mind, but as a younger child, I was always asking to hook up the plow to the mules and run them in the fields. I begged my granddad until finally he let me take out Molly and Jack. As soon as he put the straps around their shoulders, hooking them to the plow, they just took off. They knew what they were doing, and I mostly just had to run behind them to keep up. The hardest part was turning them around at the end of the field so they would go back in the other direction.

I got to plow the field that way once, but it wasn't a steady job. I did pick fruit regularly, though. The orchard on the farm was about five acres and had some apple and peach trees. There was also one big mulberry tree, which was so messy. Mulberry trees are always messy. We would put sheets on the ground around the tree and let the mulberries fall onto them. Then we would gather up the sheets and shake out the mulberries.

My grandmother and my aunt would make jam out of the mulberries. In fact, they would preserve all kinds of things in Ball jars so we'd have them for the winter—apples, peaches, peas, corn, and whatever else they raised in the garden. But I always liked picking the fruit for them because then I got a lot of nice fruit to eat while I worked.

We never had a lot of money, but people didn't buy a lot of stuff in those days anyway, just the staples: sugar and flour, salt and pepper, maybe vinegar. My granddad would take the wheat to the mill in the larger town of Concordia, twenty miles away, so my grandparents didn't have to buy flour.

My grandparents also used to make syrup out of molasses, and put it on pancakes. I hated that. I can still smell the stuff. During the war, when sugar was hard to get, that's what we used instead—that damned molasses.

Of course, they had to buy all those farm animals to start with. But because my grandparents had chickens, they didn't have to buy eggs. They had pigs, too, so they didn't have to buy bacon. They had big gardens and canned their fruits and vegetables.

We had all that and each other. We didn't need much else.

Growing up, we would have group dinners with the whole family out at the farm. Everybody would put on his best suit for dinner, except for Granddad. When we all showed up, he would be in his bib overalls. He had a suit, but he just never put it on.

We used to have homemade ice cream in the summertime, either at my grandparents' house or their neighbor Bill Holloway's place, about a half mile down the road. We'd make it in one of those old machines you had to crank by hand. We had to chip the ice by hand, too. It wasn't like you could go out and buy a bag of ice back then. You had to buy a block of ice and then use an ice pick to chip it down, bit by bit. Everybody helped. My aunt always liked to put canned pineapple in it. Talk about something good! I can still taste that ice cream—pineapple, if we had some, or vanilla. We would make that ice cream and eat it together every Sunday.

Unlike my grandparents, the Holloways had a storm cellar, so when a twister came up, we would always run over there. Growing up in Kansas, you got used to running in the summertime, because there were a lot of twisters. But my grandfather, he'd never go with us—I don't know why. He'd always say, "I'll just go to the smokehouse and wait out the storm." The smokehouse wasn't any better than the house in terms of offering protection from a tornado. I guess he just liked to be on his own when a twister came.

I don't remember any of the twisters being more than just strong winds and clouds, or sometimes we'd get a little hail. There weren't any fierce ones when I was out at my grandparents' farm, although I do remember one while I was home with my mother. She was trying to get outside so we could go to a storm cellar, but the pressure had built up so badly that she couldn't open the door. So we just stayed in the house for that one. They went by pretty quick most of the time.

In the 1940s, Haddam had a bad flood. We got about eight to ten inches of rain, and up in the creek area they had another eight or nine inches more. All that rain came down into town like a wall of water. There was a little, low-lying bridge just outside of town, running north of Main Street, and the logs and debris clogged the flow underneath it. With nowhere to go, the water just backed up right into town.

Down by the bridge was a house where an older couple lived. They had to go upstairs to get out of the water—it was that deep. The water gushed into our house, too, and into everybody's house in the part of Haddam that was flat land. The school was up on a hill, so it was okay, but for everybody in the low-lying lands, the water destroyed whatever it touched. Then, when it finally drained away, it left behind a muddy mess to clean up.

During the flood, I went outside to see what was going on. I walked uptown on one side of the street, and Carl Travers, who owned the telephone service in Haddam, was on the other side. The water was flowing along the road, and into a little culvert that had washed out. All of a sudden, Carl just disappeared. The water took him, and he went under. Thankfully, the water wasn't too deep, so he came up pretty quickly—wet but otherwise okay.

When something big like that was going on, the first thing everyone would do was turn on their radios to find out more. Tornado warnings came in over the radio, so we would keep ours on all summer long, just in case. The radio was how we got our news and a lot of our entertainment, so it was often on in the background when someone was home. Only radio though; there was no TV then.

My grandparents did have a telephone line. It was a shared line, so every family in the neighborhood who was connected to that line had their own ring. That way you knew who the call was for. My grandparent's ring, if I remember right, was one long and one short, so if it was two short rings, then we knew it was for someone else even though it would still ring on our phone. The funny thing was that everybody usually answered anyway, just to listen in. If you got a call, you could be sure somebody else was on the line eavesdropping on what you had to say.

When I was in grade school, my grandmother passed away. Then Granddad followed, several years later. I sat up with my grandfather after he died. That's how they used to do it: they would bring the body into the house so the family could mourn. They put my granddad in the living room, and my cousin and I sat up with him all night. I wasn't very old at the time, and I hadn't been exposed much to death, so spending the night with his body was pretty scary. My cousin and I talked a little bit, but people didn't seem to say as much back in those days, so mostly we just sat there. We took turns sleeping, I think. I don't remember too much about how we passed the time, but I recall feeling that it was a pretty unusual experience.

My aunt and uncle—my mom's brother, Uncle Frank, and his wife, Hazel—took over the farm after that. They got married when Hazel was really young, just thirteen years old (her dad was a mean old guy, so I think she was happy to leave home as soon as she could), but they never had any kids. After my grandparents passed away, I would still visit the farm to see them. To pass the time, I'd often go hunting for Native American relics. You could sometimes find arrowheads or hammers or other little tools in the fields, especially if you went hunting for them after it rained. Following a big downpour, it was like they would just come up out of the ground.

The only thing I ever found of any value, however, was a clay pipe. My cousin Neil Kalawoda was the real collector of Native American relics. I gave him my pipe and other stuff, because he appreciated them more than I did. He kept that stuff for years. Neil had a bone disease when he was a kid that caused one leg to be shorter than the other, so he didn't play a lot of sports or anything like that. I think that's what got him interested in collecting. I didn't have much interest in keeping such things, but I did like to hunt for them as I pictured the Native Americans camping out in our fields. Maybe there had once been a burial ground on the farm, which was why we were able to find so much stuff. What other reason could there be for so many interesting finds on my grandparents' land?

⁂

In 1933, the year I turned four, Prohibition officially ended in the United States with the passage of the Twenty-First Amendment to the U.S. Constitution. But that amendment didn't prevent states from making their own rules against alcohol, which was what happened in Kansas. It remained a dry state until 1948, longer than any other state in the union. In fact, I had left home before it became legal to drink alcohol in Kansas.

Back then, all you could get (legally) in Kansas was beer that contained 3.2 percent alcohol. That's not very much in sixteen ounces of beer. It's like drinking water. In Nebraska, you could buy a 5 percent beer and even one that was 8 percent. The authorities didn't worry about 3.2 beer because it had so little alcohol. Still, you had to have a county license to sell it. The only place around that had a license was the pool hall. That meant if someone wanted a beer, you'd usually find him at the pool hall on Main Street.

Of course, people found ways around the laws. There was a basement in this hall in the nearby town of Cuba, where you could take a bottle of something to drink. They didn't sell liquor there; you had to bring your own and sneak it down to the basement. To get a bottle, you had to find a bootlegger or go to Nebraska to buy it. Liquor was legal in Nebraska, despite funny rules about what you could buy. During the war, for some reason, you couldn't get just a bottle of something—you had to buy two bottles at once. That was just the way it was. I never could understand it.

Haddam was a small enough town that you knew everybody, so everyone knew who the bootleggers were. One guy, Mr. Lilac, would buy liquor in Nebraska and bring it across the state line. At one time, I was working at the restaurant in town for a guy named Freddie Cross, who liked to drink. Every once in a while he would say to me, "Charles, go see Mr. Lilac and get me a pint of liquor." But Mr. Lilac wouldn't give it to me, because he thought I was the one who wanted it, and I was too young to be buying liquor for myself. Freddie would have to write me a note to explain.

Of course, I wasn't buying the liquor for myself. I never had enough money to buy bootleg liquor. It was cheaper if you went to Nebraska, but the bootleg stuff cost fifty cents to a dollar more. There was not a lot of drinking back then overall—not as much as there is now—because most people couldn't afford it. They could afford to drink a glass or two of beer, but that was about it.

Once in a while, you'd hear about people getting arrested for buying liquor, but I never was worried about it. Buying it was pretty much an open secret. I went to this guy's garage one time to buy bootleg for Freddie, and he had bottles of liquor hidden all over the place. He'd be digging around through all this junk and then suddenly pull out a bottle and say, "Oh, here, I found one." They weren't visible when you walked into the garage, but they weren't hidden all that well, either, if someone cared to look. Most of the time, people bought little bottles that were easy to stash—pints or half pints, something you could stick in your pocket.

Even though drinking wasn't that big of a thing, we did have two alcoholics in town. One guy worked for Mr. Rooney, running the Ford garage on Main Street. Some days, he would visit the pool hall, drink a couple of glasses of beer, and then go back to work. That wasn't so bad, but he also had this mechanic who lived in Fairbury, Nebraska, who would bring him a bottle of whisky each day too. And this guy would drink the whole bottle. Still, you could never tell that he'd taken a drink unless you saw him do it.

The other guy had a drinking problem, but I never would have guessed because I never saw him drink. He was a good Catholic with a good family. One day, he decided to get cured, and my dad took him all the way to the hospital in Lincoln, about one hundred miles away. I remember my dad telling me that at every traffic light they saw along the road, the guy wanted to get out and have a drink. Dad had a hard time keeping him in the car, even though it was moving.

When the U.S. entered World War II, things started to change. I wasn't old enough to join up, but practically all my cousins went to war. One cousin, Bill, went off to basic training and then went straight to Europe afterward. He was there for five years. Most guys would get a furlough after they finished basic training, but he never did. He didn't get to come home until he was discharged, after the war was over.

My uncle Vic volunteered for the army and followed General George S. Patton throughout the war. He was forty years old when he signed up— about as old as you could be. Any older and they wouldn't let you serve.

In those times, if a farmer had two sons, the military might draft one and leave the other home to work the farm, so there was enough help to get the crops in. Still, a lot of farmers ended up needing extra hands from time to time. Those of us who were old enough were expected to help out. Farmers would come to the high school and say, "I want Charles, Bill, and Clyde to come to the farm today after school. We need you to work." We'd do it without question—and without getting paid. And we weren't the only source of free labor. Local farmers also used the German prisoners of war from the camp along U.S. Route 81, just north of Concordia, to work in their fields.

During the war, everything was rationed. Everyone was given stamps they had to use to buy things they needed or wanted—gas stamps, food stamps, even clothing stamps. We had a big family, so we always got a lot of stamps. People would swap stamps with their neighbors so they could get more of whatever they wanted at the time. Somebody might want extra sugar or flour to make a birthday cake one month, or extra gas stamps to take a trip somewhere. That was how it was, all over the country, because there were only limited supplies of so many things. Things started to get better as the war progressed, and it was never as bad as it had been during the drought and the Depression years.

When World War II ended, I was in Beatrice, Nebraska, with a friend, sitting in a bunk car parked along the railroad siding, where we were staying as we worked on the railroad that summer. All this noise was suddenly coming from downtown, and we couldn't figure out what the heck was going on, so we went down to see. The news had come over the radio, and the whole town started celebrating. Everyone was screaming, they were so happy. Then they broke out the liquor bottles and started partying right out in the streets. Of course, my friend and I joined in.

One of the things I remember well was how united everyone in the country was after the war. It was just the opposite of how the country is today, with people so divided about which direction the country should go. There was a common feeling of pride in being an American, pride in our country's accomplishment. I hope we can get back to that feeling one day soon.

Odd Jobs and Extracurriculars

IN A SMALL TOWN LIKE HADDAM, there isn't a whole lot going on. That's why, when I was growing up, I worked all the time. I would get bored, so for something to do, I'd get a job.

My first job was delivering the *Grit*, this little newspaper that was sold in small towns throughout the country. Unlike the *Haddam Gazette*, it had general news, not local or county news. I always thought the *Grit* was too fancy for Haddam, but I was happy to have the job—especially the delivery part. The collection part, I didn't like so much. The paper cost something like a nickel a week, but a lot of people just didn't have the extra money. I had to go door to door each week, asking people to pay up, and I often had to fight to get that five cents out of them. I didn't enjoy that at all.

After that, I did a bunch of odd jobs for different businesses along Main Street. I worked for a time at the garage, which was like a gas station with a mechanic shop set up inside. I mostly pumped gas and fixed tires. There was a lot of tire work during the war. It was impossible to get a new tire, so everybody had to patch their tires instead. I'd also wash cars for a few guys in town, who would give me a dollar per wash. That was a lot of money in those days.

Another job I had was working in the creamery. Farmers would bring in their eggs to sell, and I'd have to look at each one to make sure it was good, not rotten. One gal in particular always brought in a bunch that were rotten. I came to know whose eggs I should look at closely and whose I could trust. I'd also test the butterfat in the cream that the farmers brought to market. You determined the quality by putting a little acid in a sample. The more fat, the better—and the more money the creamery paid the farmer.

Once a week, I would have to take the cream cans down to the depot. The train ran right through Haddam back then, and it would go out on Mondays carrying farm products to different markets. We didn't have refrigerated train cars, so we chopped up blocks of ice and put the pieces around the five- or ten-gallon cream cans. But sometimes, when the weather was really hot, it wasn't enough. The butterfat would just start working, curdling in the heat, and build up energy. Then those cans would just up and explode, blowing the tops right off. Cream would go all over the place, and I'd have to mop up the greasy mess with soap and water.

When I was a freshman in high school, I started working in the pool hall for Mr. Cross—Freddie Cross's father—which may have been my most memorable job from that time in my life. During the week, I'd run the hall while Mr. Cross would go off to eat his dinner at night. Then he'd have me clean up after he closed the place. I worked all day Saturday too, and again on Sunday. I got six dollars a week for all that work.

Mr. Cross had this pill pool game going, where you'd draw a number that decided the order in which people got to shoot. Then everyone would shoot, and the winner would take the pot. I used to play for the house. Players had to beat me to get the money, but they also had to pay to be part of the game, so the house had nothing to lose. It would break even if I lost or make money if I won. And I was a pretty good pool player. I didn't get anything extra for winning, but I liked to play. Pretty much everybody played. Even kids would play pool. As I mentioned, there wasn't much else to do in town.

Another part of my job at the pool hall was to serve beer. Because the pool hall was pretty much the only place in town that had a license to sell beer, a lot of people would come in to have a keg beer or a bottle even if they weren't playing pool. This one guy who would come in, Ernie Reeser—he sure could drain a beer fast. He always ordered two beers at once. I would open up a bottle for him, and by the time I'd returned from the back with his second one, he had the first one empty. It was only 3.2 beer, but it was still funny, because I'd never seen anybody do that before.

At the time, I didn't have a driver's license—I'm not sure you even needed one in Kansas then—but once there was this guy with a car who had been drinking for so long that his friend said I had to take him home. I told the friend I'd never driven a car before. I had been behind the wheel of a tractor, but never a car. The friend told me to go ahead anyway and not to worry about it.

So I drove this guy home in his old coupe, on a gravel road, after it had rained. I hit the ditch—twice. A man happened by with his team of horses and a wagon, and he pulled me out. Both times. After I dropped the drunk guy off at home, I drove back into town. I made it okay that time, but I kept thinking it probably would have been better if he had just driven himself.

Working in that pool hall, I sure got a lesson in dealing with all sorts of people. There were these two guys who would come into town every Saturday, get to drinking beer, and then get into a fistfight. It was always about nothing, really—who was the better fighter or some nonsense like that. They would get into an argument, and then one of them would say, "Let's take this outside and settle it!"

Just northwest of the pool hall, you could cross this little bridge over a small creek on the way to the cemetery. Well, that was out of city limits, so that's where they would always go to fight. That way, they wouldn't get picked up by the sheriff. Everybody would follow them out there to watch. The two guys would hit each other a couple of times, and then they'd go back to the pool hall as friends and have another beer together. It was the craziest thing. And it happened just about every week.

I can still remember their names: Gene Kilpatrick and Andy Taylor. Andy was an ornery kind of guy, always tormenting people and looking for trouble. Once, he got into it with a man sitting in Freddie Cross's restaurant. Andy was teasing this guy, and the guy didn't like it, so he said, "I'm

going to go home to get my gun, and then I'm coming back to shoot you."
Nobody thought he was serious.

Well, I'll be damned if he didn't go home, get his gun, and come back
to shoot Andy deader than hell—point blank, right there in the restaurant,
just like he said he would. The guy went to the pen after that, for life. I
wasn't there when it happened, but I sure heard about it. Everybody in
Haddam was talking about that for a while.

When I worked in that restaurant for Freddie, I was a fry cook, I washed
dishes—every little thing you could think of. There was this ice cream
freezer, and every time I would open the door to get ice cream, I'd get the
darnedest electric shock. I just dreaded making ice cream cones for cus-
tomers because it really gave you a good jar.

Back in those days, there was a lot of fist-fighting going on. Freddie
wasn't that big of a guy, but he was one of those who could really fight.
Late one night, these two brothers came into the restaurant, and they'd
been drinking. For some reason, they wanted to take Freddie outside and
beat him up, so he went outside with them. There was a streetlight right in
the center of town, so I could see the whole thing. Freddie just whupped
them both. In a town as small as Haddam, I guess fighting was something
to do.

One summer, I worked for a guy who had bought the hotel on Main
Street and renovated it, turning it into his home on the top floor and a
grocery store on the bottom floor. I would take his pickup down to the
town of Wathena to get cantaloupes and watermelon. Then I'd sell the fruit
to the county fairs and markets when they came along. One time, I even
drove down to St. Joseph, Missouri, to pick up aspirins and other supplies
for him to sell in his store.

Most of the bigger jobs I had were summertime work, when I was out
of school. When I had just turned fifteen, I went with a friend to Wymore,
Nebraska, for the summer to work for the railroad. You had to be sixteen to

work, so I lied about my age and was hired to work on the paint gang, painting all the railroad bridges from Wymore, Nebraska, to Concordia, Kansas.

At first, they just had me painting the side of the bridge from a scaffold. Then my job changed, and I would get on this little sled that attached to the bridge's diagonal beams, lying down on my stomach, and paint the beam as I went down. It was like sliding down a banister, only I used a rope to control my speed so I wouldn't slide down too fast. I wasn't strapped in or nothing. I just had to hold on. I was usually hanging up there over a riverbed or a creek or something, but it didn't bother me. Heights never did scare me.

What did bother me was the heat. On my sled, I'd have this bucket full of paint. Well, back then they mixed the paint with creosote to make it last longer. When it got hot, the creosote would just heat up and burn my skin—mostly my face, since I was lying on my stomach with my face right in it as I painted. All summer long I painted bridges, and my face was burnt to a crisp by the end.

This old boss we had liked to taunt my friend and me. He used to say, "You young bucks! I only went through sixth grade, and look at the job I've got." My friend and I worked all summer long, staying in bunk cars—rail cars that had been converted to bunkhouses. The boss had the best car, the one with a cooking area and the whole works. Once in a while, we'd use his little kitchen, but we didn't really cook much. It was kind of like camping along the railway for the summer. We'd finish one bridge and then get in the cars and travel to the next. The bunk cars would come along with us and be parked off to the side until we were through with a bridge. Then we'd move on again. I think we painted four or five bridges that summer.

When I quit, they were about to start painting the bridge over the Missouri River. The boss wanted to hire me again, but I was able to draw something like two hundred dollars in compensation for unemployment if I stopped working and went back to school. I had to go down to the Railroad

Depot and sign up every Saturday to get my check, but it gave me pretty good spending money while I was in high school.

Working was the only way I got any money of my own growing up. Kids didn't get an allowance like they do now.

After working on the railroad all summer, I had saved all this money because it didn't hardly cost anything to live. I decided I wanted to use the money to buy some new school clothes, so I asked this trucker in town if I could ride along with him on his way to Omaha, Nebraska. He said okay, so I went to Omaha and bought some clothes. On the way back to Haddam, the trucker and I stopped in Beatrice, Nebraska, because he wanted to pick up some fresh fish. In the time it took to go down to the river, buy the fish, and come back—probably five minutes in all—somebody got in the truck and stole all my new clothes. I was sick about it. I'd used up most of my money buying them. I'd worked all summer, and somebody just took everything I'd earned in a snap.

Parents today might be pretty upset if their kids let some trucker give them a ride out of state. I was pretty independent as a teenager, as were most kids back then. It wasn't like it is now. When I went off to Nebraska for the summer at the age of fifteen with just my friend, my mom didn't think a thing about it. It was a normal thing to do. If you could get the work, you took it.

Hitchhiking was pretty common then, and often that's how I got around—that, or I got a ride with someone. My friend had a car, and one time after he'd driven us to the neighboring town of Washington for a ball game, his car broke down on the way back. So we had to walk from Washington all the way back to Haddam—about twelve miles! We were walking along the road to Haddam, waving at people and trying to get someone to pick us up, but nobody stopped. I was sure someone would recognize us and give us a ride, but no such luck. Maybe people just didn't want to pick up a couple of hitchhikers at night, but I was kind of ticked off about it.

It wasn't unusual for cars to break down in those days. We used to joke that we couldn't take a girl out on a date because the car was too filled with extra tires and the tools you needed to fix it when it broke. But that wasn't really true. I used to spend a little of the money I made going to dances, often together with a few others in somebody's car. We used to get some beer—which we weren't supposed to have at that age—and a little food, and go out to a pasture someplace and have a picnic. Then we'd all go to a nearby town to a dance.

In the town of Cuba—about nine miles from Haddam—there was a dance hall with polka dancing. We either went there or to Hubbell, Nebraska, to another big dance hall with polka music. It was always polka. One time we danced to Laurence Welk when he first started—the actual musician, not a recording. He came to Cuba with a band. Dances were a pretty big thing back then for young folks, and I always loved to dance.

Painting those bridges in the heat was probably one of the toughest jobs I ever had. To this day, I don't know how I ended up with that job. I guess nobody else wanted to do it, and I was too young to know any better. But I'm not sure it was the worst job I ever had.

Working at the grain elevator in Haddam may take that title—although not all of it was bad. Shelling corn with these two old guys was okay, except that they could really scoop corn and I couldn't. There was this big bin filled with ears of corn, and we'd have to throw them into the sheller. I was in high school, so I kept thinking, *Gosh, I'm a young guy. I can't let those guys work me to death.* But they did. They outworked me.

The corn was the good part of working at the grain elevator. The bad part was the coal. At that time, everybody burned coal for heating, so tons of it would come into the grain elevator every week by railway on this flat-bed car. My friend and I would scoop it out of the car and into a bin all by ourselves. We got paid five dollars to scoop forty tons—the entire contents of one of those flatbed cars. That was hard and dirty work.

Unloading the wheat was dirty work, too, though it wasn't as hard as shoveling coal all day. When farmers brought in their wheat, they would unload it down this shoot. The elevator would then feed the wheat into a bin. I'd have to go in that bin and level the wheat as it came in. That was the last job I did at the grain elevator. I told the owner, "If you don't have a better job than this, I quit." He didn't, so I left.

Of course, farming is really tough work, and I did a lot of that, too. In the summer, at harvest time, I used to help with thrashing the grain. I'd do what they called "spike pitching": loading up wagons with shocks of wheat or oats to be hauled back to where somebody would put them in the thrash machine. I would be out in the field doing that all day. You'd never run out of work to do because as soon as they unloaded one wagon, another one was right there, waiting to be loaded.

One of the big jobs on a farm was cleaning out the barns. That was how you'd get your fertilizer back then. Farms had a spreader and a team of horses that would take the manure and spread it in the fields. I'd help with that, with stacking hay, and with leveling off the alfalfa as it was dumped in the barn—the green alfalfa would get so hot, you had to put salt on it to keep it from setting the barn on fire.

I also got paid fifty cents per acre to shock the grain. The oats and wheat were cut, tied, and bundled with a binder, and then the grain was shocked so it would dry out. Those shocks would then be loaded onto a wagon and taken to the thrash machine to separate the grains from the straw. It was all pretty tiring work, and not that interesting after a while; it usually involved doing the same thing over and over again, all day long. When I was in high school, I did that kind of work on farms all over Haddam.

Those were the hardest jobs I had, but I didn't really have a favorite one. There was so little going on in Haddam that if an odd job was available, I usually took it—no matter what it was. I just wanted something to do that wasn't too tough. Though I didn't really understand it at the time, these experiences helped me learn the value of hard work and how to get along with all types of people. They were also the reason I usually had a little spending money in my pocket to play with.

☀

Growing up in Haddam wasn't all about work. I had some fun, too. One of the big things to do in town was listen to the prize fights on the radio. Everybody would meet at the barbershop and listen together. It was a regular thing, and we all loved it.

The fight I remember best was between the famous Joe Louis and light heavyweight Billy Conn. Louis was a heavyweight, so he was favored to win, but then Conn had him beat for all of the first thirteen rounds. They announced the points in between rounds, so we knew Conn was way ahead. All he had to do was dance for the last two rounds, and he'd have won it. But then he got too close, just for a moment, and Louis one-punched him. That was it—a knockout. We were all rooting for the underdog, so we were pretty disappointed by that one.

I never knew why we'd always meet at the barbershop for the fights. That's just how it was, for some reason. I spent more time at the barbershop listening to the fights than I did getting a haircut or a shave. They used to give shaves with a straight edge at the barbershops back then, and one of the barbers in town had kind of shaky hands. Once he got that razor on your face, his hands would go steady, thankfully.

Well, most of the time, anyway.

This one time, he dropped the straight edge on my dad and nicked his throat. Dad was bleeding all over. He was okay, but he was pretty ticked off at that barber. I never did like getting shaves at the barbershop, and that was probably why.

Back in those days, people didn't just listen to the fights on the radio. They also did a lot of boxing for fun. I had a friend who lived on a ranch north of town whose family had a boxing ring set up in their barn. His family members used to fight one another just for something to do. They wore sixteen-ounce gloves but no face guards or anything. One time, my friend and I took turns boxing his dad. He was such a good boxer, he just beat the heck out of all of us.

Sometimes, I'd go over to the high school, where there was a little gym set up in the basement for boxing and wrestling. I never got into wrestling, but I liked to box. We never had any boxing contests—just a little sparring to pass the time away.

Coon hunting was another thing the local kids did for fun. When I was young, I used to go with my friends and brothers in the wintertime. We'd take a rifle and some dogs out into the woods to see what we could find. We never did have very good hunting dogs—ours would get distracted and chase rabbits, so they'd end up running you all over the woods. I was never a very good shot either. We'd usually come home with nothing, which was disappointing.

Once in a while, though, we'd catch some coons, skin them, and sell the furs, which were worth a little extra money. One of our neighbors would even eat the meat, but most people didn't like to do that. I'm not sure why. I tasted it once, and it wasn't that bad—not nearly as bad as the time I tasted possum, which was terrible.

In my family, baseball was a popular pastime. My dad always liked baseball, so once in a while, we would go to a game on weekends. One time, I went with him and my uncles to see the Saint Louis Cardinals play (you

could also see the Saint Louis Browns back then, but we liked the Cardinals). We left early in the evening and drove all the way from Haddam—
about 450 miles on curvy, two-lane roads. This was before the interstate
highways were built, so it was really quite a drive.

We stayed Saturday and Sunday in a hotel, and came back on Monday.
It was a big deal to see a real major league baseball game. It was a big deal
to be in Saint Louis—a good-sized city, even back then. The largest town
I'd ever been to before that was Wichita. I wouldn't visit a city bigger than
Saint Louis until I left home years later.

Dad always wanted to make baseball players out of my brothers and me.
I wasn't worth a darn on the baseball field, but my brother Jim was a good
ball player—really, a great athlete all the way around, in any sport. He was
so fast, despite being pigeon-toed. Sometimes, he would get to running so
fast, he'd get tangled up in his own feet. When he got older, he was a good
softball pitcher, too. He lived in Freemont, Nebraska, and he used to pitch
all throughout the state, very seldom losing a game.

Baseball was never my sport, but while I was in school, I did play one
summer in a league in Concordia. The team paid my room and board and
gave me five dollars a week to spend. I stayed at a boarding house, and the
lady who ran it made strawberry pies for us. We'd come in all hot and sweaty
after playing all day, and the pie would be there waiting for us. I think I liked
that pie better than I liked playing baseball.

I was a pretty decent outfielder, though. I could really go back and pick
off those balls. I had a good arm and could also pitch a little bit. But it
wasn't the same for me as playing basketball. Now *that* was my sport.

I was considered a pretty good basketball player at one time, probably one
of the best in the county. (Not bragging or anything.) Everybody in town

would show up for our high school's basketball games. A lot of them followed our team to the next town, too, whenever we played there.

Our high school team was the county champion, but we never did make it to the state tournament. We won a couple of games at the regional level, but the school just wasn't big enough—we didn't have a big enough selection of players. There were only eighteen kids in my class, and half of those were girls.

I was only five-foot-eleven, and most of my teammates were that size or shorter. There weren't many players around who were over six feet tall. People just didn't grow that tall in those days for some reason. It was a different game then, in a lot of ways. For one thing, it was more of a defensive game. If you scored twenty-five or thirty points in a game, that was a lot.

My basketball coach—in grade school and then again in high school—was Mr. Law. He'd always tell the team that if they needed to make a play, they should give the ball to me. When the county school system had a free-throw shooting contest, he encouraged me to enter. He thought I had a good shot at winning, and he was right. I made twenty-three out of twenty-five free throws and walked away with a first-place medal.

Ours was a small school district, so in addition to coaching, Mr. Law taught seventh and eighth grades, and he was the principal of the grade school for a long time. He was my favorite teacher growing up, and I think I was his favorite too. He didn't just teach the fundamentals of basketball; he taught me about being a good person. I don't know how exactly, but he was able to bring out the best in people.

Mr. Law had a way of making you feel comfortable enough to say what was on your mind. I'd go to his office, and we would talk about all kinds of things. But he could also be a tough old guy. There was no monkey business on Mr. Law's team. If somebody messed around, that player would sit on the bench. Mr. Law was pretty strict that way, but I learned to appreciate it. His coaching and discipline helped me become a better player.

As a senior, I tried out for a basketball scholarship at a couple of universities. I didn't make it at Kansas State, but I was offered a small scholarship at Kansas Wesleyan in Salina, a smaller, Methodist school about a hundred miles away from home. That became my plan: after high school, I would go to college and maybe become a high school coach like Mr. Law. But that all changed when I got into a motorcycle accident.

It was my friend's motorcycle—Ben West, a kid from my class—and I was riding it around the agricultural building at school. All of a sudden, I hit a little mud puddle and the thing skidded out from under me. I smashed my foot, and that put me out of commission. I haven't been on a motorcycle since.

Ben could do anything on that motorcycle. I mean, he could really make it talk. But he was something of a daredevil too. One day, he came to school with his face all scratched up like he'd gotten into a fight with a cat. Turned out he was riding his motorcycle and slammed into his grandfather's cow. He went skidding across the gravel road, face first—killed the cow and really scraped himself up.

Years later, Ben was riding in his pickup truck along a bridge and thought he had a flat tire. He opened the door and leaned over to take a look, but he was too close to the bridge's bannister. He smashed his head, and that was it: lights out.

After my motorcycle accident, Dr. Hoover took care of me. He had a brother who was a doctor too, but the other Dr. Hoover had a little drug problem. One time, he took something that made him foam at the mouth like a mad dog. Then he attacked his wife, and she shot him! Thankfully, the Dr. Hoover who took care of me was the other one, and he was a good doctor. He had patched me up before, when I bruised my ribs playing football—he took this long, wide tape and wrapped it around me, which was some kind of misery when my sisters helped me peel it off—and again when I broke my ankle playing basketball in high school. But Dr. Hoover

wasn't able to save my chance of going to college on a basketball scholarship after my foot got smashed.

In the long run, losing that scholarship was one of the best things that
ever happened to me. If I had gone to college, I never would have met my
future wife, Jean, or had our three wonderful children. But as a young man,
of course, I didn't know that yet. I just knew I had to change my plans for
the future.

I needed a job, one with real prospects, and I knew I wasn't going to find
it in Haddam. Heck, I'd worked practically every job there was in Haddam
already. In its heyday, when Route 36 ran through town, we had around
forty businesses in all. But in the early 1940s, the highway was moved three
miles south, and it changed everything. As people traveled through Kansas, Haddam was no longer a stop along the way. We just didn't get any
traffic anymore, so by the time I finished high school, a lot of those Main
Street businesses had closed. What remained, as I recall, were the grocery
stores, a barbershop, the drug store, and a couple of gas stations. There just
weren't a lot of options for work in town anymore.

Some friends from Haddam had gone to work for the U.S. Coast and
Geodetic Survey, about seventy-five miles away in the town of Manhattan,
and they said it was a pretty good deal. Leaving town was just what most
people did when they got old enough. They'd go off to find work, just like
my dad did when I was young. The survey was hiring summer employees
at the time, so I figured I would give it a try. Once my foot healed, I went to
Manhattan and interviewed for the job.

A Short History of the U.S. Coast and Geodetic Survey

THE U.S. COAST AND GEODETIC SURVEY—once known simply as the Coast Survey—was established in 1807 by President Thomas Jefferson. Still in operation, it is the oldest scientific bureau in the nation.

Its original mission was to survey and create charts of the nation's coastline for ships to use in navigation. As the country continued to grow, the agency surveyed not just the coast but also the U.S. interior for the purposes of mapping and artillery control.

Before the Coast Survey, a haphazard system was used for surveying sites. Locals would typically survey their land or town for their own purposes, sometimes making the data available to others, sometimes not. The land survey program started so that everyone could be on the same coordinate system and all survey data would be recorded in a national network. At each point surveyed, a marker was left behind with information on how any individual could access the data by contacting the federal government.

The town of Haddam, Kansas, holds a special significance in the history of this bureau. A U.S. Coast and Geodetic Survey plaque has hung in Haddam City Hall since 1986, when it was presented to the community in recognition of the many workers the town has contributed to the survey's ranks.

The first Haddam man to join the survey was Harold Hoffman, in 1928. Many others followed, and the bottom part of the City Hall plaque lists the names of these employees from Haddam—including my own.

On the Road with the Coast and Geodetic Survey

ALL MY ODD JOBS WHILE I was growing up taught me an important lesson: when you live in a small town, any job you get is for peanuts. Working in Haddam also made me realize that I didn't want to be a farmer. I always loved my grandparents' farm, but I also knew that the local farms weren't doing very well. Most farmers had to work extremely hard just to make ends meet. By the time I was ready to graduate high school, I knew I wanted to get out of town and find someplace where I could make a better living.

The town of Haddam had become a recruiting station for the U.S. Coast and Geodetic Survey. In the 1920s, a local guy named Harold Hoffman became the first person from Haddam to join the Coast Survey. Then Lou Rogers and his brother Carl both signed up. Those three would come back to visit and talk about how they had pretty good jobs. They seemed to have more money than most, so word spread. Pretty soon, a lot of people in town wanted to work for the Coast Survey.

By 1947, when I graduated, two guys I knew—Evan Skupa and Bob McKenzie—were working for the survey. I was looking for something to do, and they encouraged me to join. I was eighteen years old when I went to Manhattan, Kansas, to interview for a summer position. That's how they did things back then: hire people for the season and then after a few months, if everything worked out, invite them to come on board permanently.

It wasn't much of an interview—just a few questions, and then the guy told me I had the job. They didn't waste any time. The operation was moving to Belleville, the next county seat to the west of Haddam, and I was told to report there Monday morning. So that's what I did.

My first job with the survey was as a signal builder. I worked with four other guys to build steel survey towers, which ranged from 37 feet to 116 feet tall. These towers looked a bit like the base of a windmill, with a scaffolding that someone could climb up. At the top was a platform where people could stand. Inside was an inner tower where we would set up the equipment used to survey the site.

I lasted through the summer and was invited to stay on. To get a permanent job, I had to take a civil service test, but it was easy—a little basic math was about all I needed for the job I was doing. But it was a very important job.

The survey party had both a day crew and a night crew. On the day crew were those of us who built the towers and tore them down; the computers who sat in their trailer and did computations to send back to the home office; the boss, usually a military guy, who oversaw the operation; and the accountant, who managed payroll, paid the bills, and kept track of spending. On the night crew were all the guys who did the observations from the towers we built.

I had been building towers for about six months when I met an employee named Joe Benge, a hotheaded little Frenchman from New Orleans who worked nights. He was just a peppy person to work with, as well as a terrible gossip. His wife, Thelma, who was a registered nurse, was even worse. Some of us on the crew used to make up stories to tell Joe, and then wait and see how long it would take him and his wife to spread them around the camp.

Well, one day Joe asked, "Charles, why don't you come work for me?"

That piqued my interest, because building towers was hard labor. We had to hoist those steel beams into place, and that wasn't even the worst part. The worst part was the digging. You had to dig anchor holes by hand. Sometimes the ground was so hard, you had to use a pick. I wasn't any good at that. Some guys have a knack for digging, but it was a struggle for me.

When Joe told me a little about the work they did on the night crew, it sounded like a much easier job. "If you can get the boss to approve it," I told him, "I'd be glad to work with you."

The boss said okay, so that's how I moved from the labor side of things and started learning how to become a surveyor.

At night, we'd go up to the top of those towers I'd been building with the day crew. Light keepers on each tower would shine lights at the observers waiting on top of other towers, and the observers were able to take their angles and measurements. You couldn't work during the day because there would be too much refraction to get an accurate reading. So we always worked at night, when the light shone clearly, with no interference (most of the time). The observers would sit there all night long, taking measurements in all directions. Then all that data would be computed to determine accurate coordinates for the site.

Joe was an observer, so he would use the survey equipment to take the readings. I was the recorder, so I would sit next to him and record his observations. Basically, he'd read off numbers, and I'd write them down. At the end of the night, I'd help him do the calculations that we had to turn in to the office. I was able to learn how things worked on the job, and it wasn't long before I was doing observations myself.

When I joined the Coast Survey, the federal government had probably five survey parties going on at one time, at various points all over the United States. Level parties measured and recorded the elevation at different places. Gravity parties measured the variations in gravitational pull from place to place. Astronomical parties recorded the positioning of the stars. And triangulation parties worked to figure the exact coordinates of a certain point by measuring the angles to it from known points on either side of a fixed baseline. That's the kind of party I was on. There were triangulation parties on the East Coast, on the West Coast, and in the Midwest, where I was located most of the time. It was a huge operation.

When I started working as part of the night crew, my triangulation party was still located in Belleville, but we soon moved on to other locations in Kansas, such as Oberlin and Dodge City. Every time we were assigned a new location to survey, we picked up and moved everything with us. We always lived within about a fifty-mile radius of the survey site, because the government didn't want us to have to travel too far to get to work. Because the goal was to survey the entire country, we had only about thirty days to survey each area before we moved on to the next one.

I remember my salary when I started, including a per diem of two dollars per day for living expenses, was two hundred dollars a month. An accountant traveled with us, who wrote all the checks to suppliers and gave out payroll. Your paycheck wouldn't come in the mail or get deposited automatically the way it's done today. Instead, everyone lined up on Friday, and the accountant just handed us a check. He always made arrangements with a local bank, giving our names so the bank would cash our checks for us.

The accountant worked out of a trailer along with the boss, set up near the trailer where the computers worked and another one that held supplies for the day crew. Working out of trailers made our operation mobile. The long-term personnel lived out of their own trailers, which they drove from site to site using a government vehicle. I didn't get one of those until after I was married. When I started out, I usually got a room at a boardinghouse or motel near the survey site.

When our caravan of trucks and trailers arrived in a new town, it created quite a stir. We usually drove in together, this big line of vehicles—some gray, others bright orange—so we were hard to miss. When we first got to a new town, people wondered what we were doing there, but most of the time they were glad to have us. After all, the survey team would spend lots of money in town, so the local businesspeople were always glad about that. Everybody treated us pretty well. At a restaurant or bar, it was like we had lived there our whole lives.

Every time we moved, somebody would go ahead to find a place where we could set up. We didn't have to figure out any of that for ourselves. Somebody always just told us where to go. When we got there, only one person—the accountant—was paying the bills, so anyone, like a mechanic, could just go out and buy parts he needed and put them on the account. None of us had to handle any money. We worked for the federal government, so anytime we needed supplies from a business in town, that business could be assured it was going to get paid. There was a system in place, and it worked like clockwork.

─☼─

When I first started with the Coast Survey, a crew of about forty or fifty people traveled together from place to place, including workers and their families. It wasn't hard to live together as a community, because everybody had a job to do and most of us liked the work. It was amazing how well we all got along—a few arguments among some of the younger guys from time to time, when they were off work and had too much to drink, but that was about the worst of it. A couple of military guys might challenge each other once in a while—you might have a marine and an army soldier who would get into it a little bit—but it wasn't work-related most of the time, and it never amounted to much.

The survey crew was a mixed group, a whole range of ages. Some guys traveled with their families, kids and all; others were single guys like me. Because we lived and worked so close together, it was easy to get to know people, and I made some good friends.

I liked my first boss a lot: Bob Engdahl. He was just a good person, a civil engineer from Minnesota who lived in a trailer along with his wife and two girls. We used to play poker together, a game that Bob loved. One time, he had a decent hand, three aces, and another guy had three tens. Both thought they were sitting pretty and didn't notice that I had a small straight going. I just needed one more card, so I kept sticking. They should have run me out, but they got cocky. Finally, I hit that straight and threw all my money in the pot. Bob was so pissed off at me for taking him out that he was pretty cold to me for a while—he just wouldn't forget about it. Some of those guys sure were serious about their poker.

The crew got along for the most part, even though there sure were some characters. One guy, Miles Lundy, used to sleep with his eyes open. No joke. One time, when we were working in Osceola, Missouri, Lundy was sharing a tent with Alvin Woods, another guy from the party. They'd go to the local barbershop for a shower when they needed one (you could do that back then) and just use the tent for sleeping. After they'd been drinking a while one night after work, Lundy left Alvin at the bar, went back to the tent, and fell asleep. A while later, here comes old Al—he'd had too much to drink, and he saw Lundy lying there on his cot, eyes wide open. Al got all upset and ran straight to town, shouting for the undertaker, sure that Lundy was dead.

Of course, when the undertaker arrived in his hearse and tried to pick up the corpse, Lundy woke right up and started howling. That was when Al realized his mistake.

Another memorable guy was T. J. Mills from Somerset, Kentucky. I spent about a week with him one time when he was sent along to help me in Kansas—long enough to learn how to imitate the way he talked (though I lost that talent somewhere along the way). He had a stutter, which wasn't a problem. What *was* a problem was working outside in the cold of December, when T. J. wouldn't wear more than a light jacket. I kept some warmer clothes in the truck, but he just wouldn't put them on. He wanted to tough it out, I guess, but it wasn't easy to watch him sitting there, looking so cold while we worked.

I made some good friends when I was with the Coast Survey: Frank Fencel, a former army mechanic who was from Haddam like me, and Hubert Twaddle, whose job was to haul steel out to the area where we were going to build a tower. We kept in touch for years, even after both those guys left the survey and headed home—Frank back to Kansas to farm, and Hubert to Missouri, where he became a mail carrier.

As far as bosses went, Bob was probably the best out of all of them. On the surveys, bosses came and went. The government typically sent out junior officers—engineers or mathematicians—to take over for just two years or so. For them, this was a training period in geodetic survey. Afterward, they'd move on to something else, and the government would send along another new officer. These officers were usually pretty young, so often it was the older employees on the survey party who ended up training the bosses in the work we did.

Some bosses I didn't like too much, but others were really nice guys. Ray Spears, whom I liked a lot, was from Lubbock, Texas, and later became an admiral in the NOAA NOS-NGS officer core. Every once in a while, some of us would get in the car and do what we called a "beer can traverse"— driving around the county, drinking beer. Ray and I decided to do that one Friday in Kimball, Nebraska, when we'd had enough of it all and needed to get out for a while. He was better than most bosses—not so formal. Unlike the others, he could just let go of things and say, "To heck with it!"

―――

Surveying work wasn't for everyone. The reason the government hired people and tried them out on a temporary basis was simple: a lot of them didn't last. Some people just couldn't stand heights, for example, so working on top of those towers wasn't for them. From time to time, guys were sent out from Washington—maybe a congressman's son or someone—who wouldn't last the summer. The work was too tough, or they didn't like living on the road. A lot of people didn't want to work at night.

When I moved to the night crew, we'd usually start around four or five o'clock in the evening, just about the time most people would be knocking off work. We would drive or hike out to the survey site, depending on where it was, and get everything set up before the sun went down. We'd write up a description of how to get there, starting from a certain point in town or wherever, so someone coming after us could locate the markers and reach the site. You wanted all your groundwork finished and all your equipment ready so you could start your observations as soon as it got dark. Then we'd work several hours at night taking readings before heading back to home base. We had a job to do, and it didn't matter if it took one hour or ten hours. We would work until it was completed.

When you got on top of one of those towers at night, it worked like this: An observer had a theodolite, a specialized instrument used in surveying to measure angles. When I first started, I used a Parkhurst theodolite, which had a scope and micrometer knobs on the side for making adjustments. Once the instrument was set up, you would look through the scope and aim the crosshairs at the point to be measured. You could then record both vertical and horizontal angles. The theodolite sat on a 360-degree plate with etchings all the way around it, and you would go around the circle, measuring the angles to the designated point from each etched mark.

Then, using triangulation, you would compute the distance and direction for each side of the triangle. In that way, you were able to determine the latitude and longitude of the point being measured. The coordinates would be recorded in a national database, and people could use them to make active surveys or topographic maps, test satellites, and later for the global positioning system, or GPS—a technology that was just being tested when I retired in the 1980s.

That Parkhurst theodolite was a bit tricky. Lining it up properly required the observer to make several adjustments on the micrometer and the level. Often, it wouldn't stay fixed, so you were constantly having to adjust it. Plus, it took two people to operate the instrument. The observer would use the A micrometer, or mic, to read one side of the plate, while another person used the B mic to read the other side. Not long after I started with the Coast Survey, the government sent us a Wild T3 instead, which one person could operate alone. It was also more precise, required less adjustment, and was easier to use, so that made the job a little less difficult.

Using the equipment—even the Parkhurst—wasn't that hard, but it took some practice. As a recorder, I first learned by watching the observers I worked with, and then I took it upon myself to practice and learn how to do new things. I read up on what might be the cause of an incorrect reading and what you could do to fix such errors. But most of what I learned just came from experience out in the field.

Because you had to work your way up to being an observer, most people were pretty competent by the time they got to that stage. Everybody had to climb up the same career ladder, and that process worked pretty well. If you weren't cut out for that kind of work, you just wouldn't make it that far.

You never really knew how long a job would last until you got there. It often depended on the weather. Weather was our biggest obstacle—wind, rain, and fog all made it so you couldn't take accurate readings. Clouds weren't a big problem in places like Kansas, where it's flat, but when we did surveys in the mountains, clouds might come down right over the top of you. All you could do then was sit there and wait for the clouds to move on. The same was true when there was a big storm. One time when we were in Minnesota, a twister went through. You could hear it coming, like a train coming through town. That was probably the most severe storm I encountered, but luckily, it didn't do much damage.

Another time, in Pattonsburg, Missouri, a storm came through with severe winds. We had a mechanic on the team, Lawrence Roberts, who sometimes pitched a tent to work out of. In Pattonsburg, he set it up on a hill to do some work on a Dodge ambulance that had been used during the war—one of many former military vehicles that the government sent us to use on our field party. So Lawrence put that old ambulance up on stands in his tent, and then he went off to town for some parts he needed to fix it. That's when the storm came up—so strong that it blew that ambulance right off the stands, out of the tent, and all the way down the hill.

Lawrence came back scratching his head, wondering where the ambulance had gone. At last, he found it all the way down the hill, in a ditch.

Our crew set up in Gorham, New Hampshire, at one point so we could survey an area that included Mount Washington. Someone once told me that the top of Mount Washington is the coldest place in the world. I don't know if that's true, but I read that the strongest winds ever observed were recorded atop that peak, which held the world's record at the time our team set up there. We had a thirty-seven-foot tower on Mount Washington when we were working there, and the wind beating against that tower was so fierce that we had to secure it with log chains so it wouldn't blow over.

Mount Washington experiences terrific ice storms, too. The ice collecting on that tower got so heavy one day that the whole tower collapsed. Thankfully, nobody was on it at the time—the weather was too bad for us to get any work done.

One day in Gorham, when we were all sitting around the office, someone said, "Who wants to go to Mount Washington?" No one said a word.

We all preferred to stay down in the Gorham area, where there wasn't so much weather to deal with. I was working as an observer at that point, and I knew there was only one guy for the job. "Send Bud," I said. "He'll go anyplace, anytime. He'll do anything." I was talking about Marvin Randall. He was the type of guy who didn't care about nothing but getting the job done. So that's who was sent up the mountain, and true to his reputation, he got the job done.

Once Bud and I were working someplace together, and he was in charge of the night observations. It was his job to make sure everything happened the way it was supposed to. So one night, he was working on one tower and I was on another across the way. But it was so windy that night, I didn't bother to get set up. Most of the time, when the sun goes down, the wind goes down. That wasn't always the case, but it was generally the rule we went by. And if the wind was really blowing, everything would move around on top of the tower—sometimes even the tower itself would rock. You just couldn't take accurate readings under those conditions.

On this particular night, my recorder and I could see Bud on his tower, running around and setting up his equipment. We used our lights to flash him a message by Morse code—that was how we communicated with guys on the other towers. We told him we were going to wait for the wind to die down before we got started.

"Don't wait," he responded. "Go ahead and get set up."

By that time, I had a lot of experience on these towers. "I'll set up when I'm ready," I told my recorder. "Tell Bud to just go to hell." I really meant it, too. I was going to get the job done if it was feasible, but I wasn't going to waste my energy when the wind was blowing like that.

Well, the next day when I went by the office—boy, was he ticked off at me! I thought, *God, I might get fired.* Bud was the one in charge, after all. But he cooled down. I like to think that once he had a chance to think about it, he knew I was right.

Despite always being out in all types of weather, I never was afraid to work on the survey. I never really thought of it as dangerous work, even when I was climbing the highest towers. The highest ones were 116 feet tall, but they were used only in the flat country, like in Louisiana, where you had to get up over the trees in order to see the horizon so you could account for the curvature of the earth. If you were already up on a mountainside, you didn't need a tower that size; you might have nothing more than a small stand to put your equipment on.

Of course, the Coast Survey parties had their mishaps. Oftentimes, we had to hike through rough terrain to reach our survey site. It was up to us surveyors to figure out the way there and, just as important, the way back. Usually, we'd bring a hatchet along and blaze trees with an X to mark our route. Some guys would bring toilet paper to leave behind as trail markers, but I never thought that was a good idea. If it rained, those strips of paper would just wash away. We'd usually be hiking out of these places in the dark of night, so we needed to make sure we could really see our markers. We always had flashlights, but sometimes that wasn't enough.

Once, when we were in northern Michigan, up around Marquette, a survey party got lost. They were heading back at night and walked right off the wrong side of a mountain. We had no radios at that time, so they didn't have any way to call for help. What's more, no one was looking for them because no one knew they were missing. If they hadn't found their way to a road eventually and run into somebody who was able to help, they could have been out there for a long time. Nothing like that ever happened to me, though. I was always careful about blazing my trail.

There was the occasional accident as well. One time, this kid from Arkansas, Edward Word, was riding a little Indian pony on top of a mountain in the vicinity of Taos, New Mexico, when all of a sudden that horse's foot went right in a hole. The horse went down, and I thought, *Oh my God! Ed's got to be hurt.* But neither Ed nor the horse was hurt at all. They just took a pretty good jar.

In Manhattan, Kansas, we had a guy working with us who had a deformed right arm: Max Schaffer. Max wasn't able to use that right arm for much, so he did most things with his left, including climb those towers, put the lights on them, and direct the lights at the survey party. And he could do it as well as anyone. But one day, he fell off the tower.

Now, Max was as strong as an ox. With just one good arm, he would shoot horseshoes (one of my favorite pastimes with the field team) and win pretty consistently. I was one of the best pitchers in our group—when my family gets together from time to time and plays cornhole, I'm grateful for all the time I spent pitching horseshoes back in the day. The only person I couldn't beat was Max. He could throw the horseshoes two or three feet off the ground, getting ringers most of the time. Once, I managed to win two out of three games, and Max was pretty upset about it. He didn't like losing. We played many times after that, and I never won again. That's how good he was.

So I never was sure of exactly why Max fell. He probably just slipped. No safety nets were used with the towers then, so if a person slipped, he had better catch on to something or he'd fall to the ground. By chance, Max landed in the soft dirt that had just been dug up around the anchors supporting one leg of the tower. That dirt braced his fall and probably saved his life. He walked away with only a few scratches from where he hit the tower steps on his way down. Still, I don't think Max ever climbed those towers again.

We had another guy who wasn't so lucky. He fell backward into the center of a tower in Minnesota, from about seventy-seven feet up. After rattling against the sides of the tower on his way down, he hit the bottom pretty hard. The poor guy hurt his back and was in bad shape for a while, but he made it. And once, when a party was tearing down a tower, some-body threw down a light plate—the piece of metal where the lights were attached—and hit a guy in the head. It didn't kill him, but it did some real damage to his brain. He had to stop working and never was right after that.

At one point, the survey workers tried to unionize. The idea was to make the towers safer to build and climb on. They wanted to build a cage around the ladder leg, for example, so that if you fell back, you had some-thing to grab on to before you tumbled all the way to the ground. It was a good idea, but it didn't work. Building towers that way would have taken longer and cost more money, so I guess the government didn't think that unionizing was such a good idea.

Despite it all, I loved working with the Coast Survey from the start. By the end of my time with the survey, I would make my home in more than sixty towns throughout the country, mostly in the Midwest. I would go from being a single guy living on my own to having a wife and three kids who traveled with me. There were a lot of changes during that time—both for me personally and for the entire country.

A Short History of Meadville, Missouri
39° 47' 12" N, 93° 18' 10" W

MEADVILLE IS A SMALL TOWN IN Linn County, in northern Missouri. It has never had more than a few hundred people living there, at least not since the government started taking the census. The town got its name from Charles Mead, a representative of the St. Joseph Railroad, and in fact dates back to the completion of the Hannibal and St. Joseph Railroad line through the county in the mid-1800s.

Besides being the birthplace of my wife, Dorothy Jean Siegrist, Meadville is home to the historic Locust Creek Covered Bridge, located just north of town. Built in 1868, it is the longest covered bridge (151 feet) still standing in the state of Missouri. At the time it was built, it connected the main east–west road in northern Missouri and was part of one of the nation's first transcontinental roads.

Although it's no longer on a main artery through the state, the bridge has become a State Historic Site and is preserved by the Missouri Department of Natural Resources.

A Whirlwind Romance

IT WAS 1948, AND I WAS nineteen years old. I had worked with the survey for about a year when we landed in Chillicothe. Located in northwest Missouri near the Grand River, the town of Chillicothe (39° 47' 35" N, 93° 33' 07" W) was named by the Shawnee people, who originally settled the area. It means "big town where we live," even though it wasn't so big when I lived there. But it wasn't so small either—maybe around eight thousand people lived there permanently, and people were always coming through because it was located at the intersection of highways 36 and 65.

At the time, I had a good friend named Andy Brown, who was famous for his whistling. He could whistle just like a bluebird. One night when we weren't working, we decided to go into town and have a beer at this place called the Triple H. We were sitting there with our beers when we noticed four girls sitting in a booth across the way. Andy said to me, "Charles, go ask one of those girls to dance."

So I went up and asked one of them to dance. Her name was Jean. It has always been a mystery to me why I picked Jean out of the four girls. The other three weren't too bad either. Maybe it was all about location: she was sitting on the inside of the booth, where I could see her best. Whatever the reason, it didn't matter. She immediately turned me down.

I was kind of upset about that, but she just didn't want to dance. So I went back to my table. I learned later that after I left, Jean's friends told her she was nuts, that she should have danced with me.

When I told Andy what had happened, he wasn't having any of it. "Why don't you go ask her again?" he said.

I told him I wasn't going to do that. I wasn't used to being turned down, and I certainly didn't want to go get turned down a second time. But he kept nudging me until finally I went back and asked her again. And this time she said yes.

There was a band playing modern music—"Slow Boat to China" and that kind of stuff. Back in those days, that's what we used to dance to. So I took Jean out on the dance floor and did a light shuffle with her. Then I looked into her beautiful green eyes, and I was hooked. I knew she was the one for me.

It turned out that Jean and her friends had been at a bankers' convention that evening and stopped by the Triple H afterward. Jean worked for the Citizens Bank in Chillicothe. She hadn't wanted to go out afterward, but her friends had talked her into it, saying, "Don't be a killjoy." She gave in and joined them, and it was a good thing that she did. Once I got her to say yes, we danced the rest of the evening together.

We talked as we danced, and the conversation was just easy, really easy. At first, Jean thought I was older than she was, but I wasn't much older—just a few months. When she saw the high school ring I was wearing, she realized we had graduated the same year. She told me she didn't usually date guys her own age, but she must have liked me well enough by the end of the night. Otherwise, why would she have agreed to have lunch with me the very next day?

After I picked Jean up for lunch, we went to what was probably the cheapest restaurant in town. I didn't have a lot of money, but it didn't seem to matter. Lunch went so well that I asked her for another date. I was already getting that feeling, you know? It just seemed like we were really hitting it off.

I don't know how I knew exactly that Jean was the one for me, but I did. I had dated several girls, but most of them had been silly. None of them were as intelligent as Jean. She was smart and easy to get along with, and she was cute. She seemed to think I was pretty okay too. I used to wear these turtleneck sweaters back then—yellow or red—and I had one of those on when I took her to lunch. She thought I was pretty handsome in that turtleneck.

The crew I worked with got wind of the news pretty quickly that I had started dating a girl who worked at the bank. Jean was in the loan department most of the time, but she often worked as a teller during the lunch hour, when there was the most traffic. A bunch of the guys went down to the bank at lunchtime and lined up in front of Jean's window even though there were two other tellers working and no one in line at their windows. They wanted to get a look at her.

I didn't have anything to do with that—I didn't even know they were going down there—but Jean wasn't too happy about it. She kept dating me all the same, which I took as a good sign.

Sometime that summer, Jean took me out to her parents' farm for an introduction. She grew up in Meadville, Missouri, a little bitty town of just a few hundred people located about fifteen miles east of Chillicothe. Her dad had been married before, but lost his first wife just before the Depression and then married her mother. Jean's mother had been a teacher, and her dad had gone to Chillicothe Business College for a while. He had quit because his own dad needed help on his farm, and he never did get a chance to go back and finish college.

Jean grew up on the farm her dad bought just before the crash came in 1929. Unlike many people at the time, he was able to hold on to his farm during the Depression, but it was rough going in the early days. Her family wasn't so different from mine, really. They didn't have any money during that time, but nobody did, so it didn't matter much.

There was always plenty to eat on the family farm. They grew corn, soybeans, and lots of oats, and they raised all sorts of animals—cows, pigs, sheep. Jean even had a pet sheep when she was young. Its mother had rejected it, so Jean would feed it with a bottle. She and her sister took care of that pet all summer long, until it was old enough to get by on its own.

I was surprised by how much meat they ate at Jean's house. They butchered their own livestock and kept it in a meat locker in town. I was at her house one time when her mother brought out a big platter of T-bone steaks. I wasn't used to seeing a pile of steaks like that, so I said, "How many people are going to eat all that?" It seemed like way more than we needed, but I ate two of those T-bones because I knew what would happen if I didn't: she'd throw the rest of them to the dog, because Jean's family didn't eat leftovers. And that's exactly what happened. The rest of them went to her dad's little black dog. I sure was glad I ate that second steak.

Jean got the job at the bank in Chillicothe just after graduating from high school. She had two older sisters in college at the time, so her dad had told her, "Jean, I can't help you too much because I couldn't help the other girls. It wouldn't be fair." That was okay with her. She was just interested in seeing what it was like to be on her own for a while, so she got the job at the bank and moved to Chillicothe to live with a friend.

I still remember where she lived—at 4 Cherry Street, just down the way from the bank, so she could walk to work. I didn't have a car then, so I used my friend's car, a 1941 Oldsmobile (which I thought was a pretty good car) whenever I would pick her up for a date. We went on the kinds of dates that most people went on back then: to the movie theater in town, out to dinner, to a dance or two. That was about all we had time for. Pretty soon, I would be leaving town.

Jean and I started dating in the summertime. By the holidays, the survey was finishing up the job in Chillicothe, and we were about ready to move. We were heading to Texas right after Christmas, and I wanted to take Jean with me.

Just before Thanksgiving, I bought a ring in a jewelry store in town—a keepsake diamond, which was pretty well known at that time. Then I asked

Jean if she wanted to marry me. We had discussed the idea of marriage already, so I didn't have to do a lot of convincing. She knew she'd be traveling with me, and she didn't have any problem with that. She was kind of excited about it.

She said yes, so then we both had to go home and tell our parents the news over the Thanksgiving holiday. Jean's folks thought she had lost her mind. Not only was she marrying a man they barely knew, but he would be taking her all the way to Texas in just a month's time. Jean told me later that her mother was calm throughout the conversation, but her dad was a different story. He didn't yell or anything, but he was very upset that she wanted to marry someone she had just met. He thought that it was too soon, that she might be making a terrible mistake.

My parents had a similar reaction to Jean's: My mother didn't really say anything. My dad thought I was crazy. I was the first of my siblings to get married, so it came as a real surprise.

"You know, you're going to be married a long time," my dad said. That was his way of warning me that this was a decision I was going to have to live with.

I wasn't concerned. "Just don't worry about it," I told him. "I'll take care of things. I'm not going to be asking you for anything."

That was the end of it. He never mentioned it again after that. And he was right about it being a decision to last a lifetime: Jean and I have been married nearly seventy years.

⁂

After the Thanksgiving holiday, we didn't have much time to prepare. I had to be in Texas for work right after Christmas, so we decided to get married on Christmas Eve.

Before Jean and I could be married, we had to get blood tests and then get a license. We did all that in Haddam so she could have a chance to meet my family. Other than that, we didn't make any big plans. We just wanted to make it official in time for her to come to Texas with me, so that's what we did.

A few days before our wedding, I picked Jean up at her parents' house. She and her dad were always very close, and when he was telling her good-bye, he leaned in and said, "You know, Jean, you can come home anytime." I guess he figured that things might not work out between us. We went back to Meadville for a visit the following spring, and her dad and I got along just fine, but at that moment he wasn't so sure about me.

Jean and I drove off on our own after that. As we were riding along, I stopped the car at the intersection with Route 36, about three miles south of Haddam. At that intersection, you can turn left to go back to Meadville, or you can turn right and head to Belleville, where we planned to get mar-ried. I turned to Jean and asked her which way she wanted to go. I wanted to know if she was certain about her choice. Did she want to go back home to her parents, or go ahead and get married?

Well, she chose the right way. We got married in a little Methodist church in Belleville on December 24, 1948. Her parents didn't come to the wedding ceremony—mine didn't either, but that wasn't unusual in those days. My older sister, Donna, and my best friend at the time, Frank Fencel, stood up for us, and that was it—just the four of us and the preacher.

It really was a whirlwind wedding. We'd known each other for just a few months. She was only eighteen, still a month away from her nineteenth birthday, and I was only nineteen myself. Looking back, it's hard to believe how young we were, but we didn't have any sense of it then. We fell in love, and we didn't really know what we were getting into, but it didn't matter. It all worked out in the end.

It was such a whirlwind, in fact, that I'm still not quite sure it actually happened. I know we went to the church and said *I do*, but we never did get a copy of our marriage certificate. I'm pretty sure the preacher signed all the paperwork, but to this day, I don't know if it was registered properly.

Every time I went home to Haddam for a visit, I kept thinking I should go over to the courthouse to make sure we were official. Somehow, I never got around to it, and after we'd been married for seven or eight years, I figured, who cares? It may well be that we've just been shacking up all these years, but if that's true, it doesn't seem to have made a whole lot of difference.

Jean and me on our wedding day, December 24, 1948

━✴︎━

I had to be back at work a few days after Christmas, and it would take two days to drive down to southern Texas from Kansas. So after we got married, we had to leave almost right away.

We returned to my parents' home with plans to leave for our honeymoon that same day. But even before we left the church in Belleville, it had started snowing. By the time we got back to Haddam, the storm was taking over. We were snowed in the rest of the night, and gosh, it was cold. People always jokingly ask, "How was your wedding night?" We can honestly say that ours wasn't all that good! We spent two very cold days at my parents' house before the snow cleared up enough that we could leave.

I ended up working in so many places in Texas during my time as a surveyor that I can't remember which southern Texas town we went to first—it might have been Corrigan or Grafton or Raymondville—but I do remember that we stayed in a little apartment there that I had rented from a lady. It wasn't anything fancy: just a bed, a stove, a table, and two chairs. Jean and I didn't have much money to speak of, so that was all we could afford.

Jean had a hundred dollars that she'd inherited from her grandmother. It wasn't even her true grandmother, but the mother of her father's first wife. Still, she had left a little money to Jean all the same, and it was lucky for us that she did. Otherwise, we'd have started out with little more than the clothes on our backs.

Even though we'd both been working, neither of us had saved that much. I had stashed away a little before ending up in Chillicothe, but I didn't have much left after buying Jean's engagement ring. (We don't even have that ring anymore. Years ago, it went down the garbage disposal and was lost for good.) Jean had spent most of what she earned on nice clothes for work, but of course she didn't need those fancy clothes on the road, so she left most of them behind. I had spent my money on clothes too—and also beer. The money didn't really go that far then, because we weren't making very much. Even still, we could have saved a little to prepare for married life, but I don't think either of us thought much about it until after our wedding. But soon enough, Jean started planning for our future, and then I started saving for sure.

Back then, it cost us only about five dollars a week to eat. We cooked meals for ourselves in our little apartment, and I soon learned Jean couldn't boil water. I figured that having married a farm girl, I was in for some good cooking. In my house growing up, my mom always made us help out in the kitchen. My brothers and I even had to do all the dishes after each meal. That wasn't the case with Jean's mother. She was a really good cook, but she liked to do everything herself. She never enlisted Jean's help, so Jean never learned to make a thing.

Despite that little hiccup, Jean took to life with me on the road pretty quickly. She liked the adventure of it. She liked seeing new places. She liked the people on the Coast Survey who traveled with us. She really liked that there was always someone around to go out with on a Saturday night. That's one of the perks of traveling from place to place with your friends.

I guess if it hadn't worked out, Jean and I could have always blamed Andy Brown. He was the one responsible for getting us together in the first place, because if he hadn't made me go back and ask Jean to dance a second time, that would've been the end of it. None of this would have happened, and my life would have been very different. The funny thing is, Andy never even thought to ask one of the girls to dance. He was just interested in making sure that I got to dance with the girl I wanted. And lucky for me that he was.

A Short History of
Tucumcari, New Mexico
35° 10' 10" N, 103° 43' 32" W

LOCATED IN QUAY COUNTY, IN NORTHEASTERN New Mexico, the town of Tucumcari was founded in 1901 as a construction camp while the railroads were being built. First called Ragtown, and then known as Six-Shooter Siding because of all the gunfights it saw, the town was renamed Tucumcari, after nearby Tucumcari Mountain, when it became a permanent settlement in 1908.

The population of Tucumcari was approximately eight thousand people when I lived there with the Coast and Geodetic Survey in the 1950s; in the 2010 census, that figure had dropped to 5,363. The town was situated on the Old Route 66 (now Interstate 40), or what locals called the Mother Road, which was made famous in the song "(Get Your Kicks on) Route 66."

Although Tucumcari was known as "the town that's two blocks wide and two miles long," an ad campaign nonetheless boasted about the sheer number of rooms available within that small area, with road signs that read: *Tucumcari Tonite! 2,000 Motel Rooms.* The main drag was crowded with gas stations, motels, and restaurants—many of which can still be seen today.

Small-Town Life

SOON AFTER WE WERE MARRIED, JEAN and I decided we didn't want kids right off the start. Instead, we wanted time. We wanted to celebrate our own lives a little bit—and our lives together. That meant we were free to do whatever we wanted to.

I never will forget the time in 1949, not long after we were married, when a guy on the survey crew was going down to some little town in Texas, not far from where we were staying.

"I've got a friend down there who's building his own television set," he said. "Why don't you come along and see?"

Back then, you could send away for a kit in the mail, and then you could put the TV together yourself. That's what this guy was doing, and everyone wanted to get a look at it. That was the first television Jean and I had ever seen. Having your own TV set was a big deal then.

Jean didn't work during those first years as newlyweds, because we never stayed anywhere long enough for her to get a job. We were in each town for only about a month or so before we moved on. She'd been used to working every day, but she didn't mind the change. She quickly made friends with the wives of the other men in the field party. While I worked, she spent time with them, or she read. That was when she finally learned to cook, too.

Having our friends with us made it easier to move from place to place. We did most everything as a group. Sometimes we'd gather at someone's trailer and play cards—there was a lot of card playing back in those days.

My boss, Bob Engdahl, and his wife were regular card players. When I was working at night, Jean was often Bob's partner in pinochle. He always wanted Jean to cheat, because he didn't like to lose. I'm proud to say she just wouldn't do it.

We often went out as a group, too. Most of the towns where we worked were pretty much the same—similar to Haddam, except the scale might be a little different. Some towns were larger, some were smaller, but they all had the same basic things to offer as any other midwestern town: a main street where you could find a gas station, a barbershop, and a general store, maybe a bar or two, and a place where you could get dinner. Most of these small towns had a movie theater, and a lot of them had drive-ins. Jean and I would go into town with friends just about every week, whether to the movies, to dinner, or to have a beer.

We'd also go to dances together as a group. No matter what small town we were in, you could pretty much count on there being a dance, usually on Saturday nights. Back in those days, people would take their whole families to the dances, kids and all. We did that just about every week, too.

The dances were pretty similar from town to town, whether you were in Minnesota, Kansas, or Texas, but a few stood out to me. At one dance hall in a little bar out in the Texas countryside, in the town of Grafton, there was sawdust on the floor and the band played with a washboard and a broom as instruments. One guy would make the broom scratch the floor, and another would strum the washboard like it was a guitar. They were actually pretty good.

After the dances, we'd usually leave at around eleven or twelve o'clock at night, all together. We would stop somewhere to eat a middle-of-the-night breakfast on the way home.

Working with the survey party really was like having one big family that worked, played, and traveled together. We knew everybody in the party, and everybody was pretty close. If you needed something, somebody was always there to help you out. When you landed in a new place, someone would always go out and explore with you. Jean and I both discovered pretty quickly that we liked traveling and living this way.

It was a good thing that we had this family-like group to travel with, because once we left Missouri, we didn't have a chance to visit our parents very often. I only got vacation time once or twice a year, so we'd go home to visit Jean's family around the holidays and maybe again in the summer as well. We used to stop by my folks' place once in a while, but more often, we would go to one of Jean's family reunions. Like most women, Jean had priorities.

Our family didn't often come to visit us, although Jean's father and mother met up with us one time when we were in Carrollton, Missouri, about fifty miles from Meadville. They didn't stay overnight—just came out for the day and drove home in the evening. Two of Jean's sisters, her brother, and a cousin stopped by to see us at various times when we were living in different areas of the country, but visits of this sort weren't a regular thing.

Thankfully, after their initial concern about us getting married so young, Jean's family took to me pretty quickly. When we visited, I'd always go out with Jean's dad to help out around the farm. One time I was milking a cow, and it stepped right in the bucket, spilling the milk all over the place. Her dad said it was a good thing I had my job with the government, because he didn't think farming was the right profession for me.

Another time, I helped Jean's dad put a fence around the earth pond. People used to build these ponds that had a tank with water for the cattle, but you had to have a fence around the pond so the cattle wouldn't just drop in there. So I was trying to hammer in a staple to hold barbed wire to the fence post, but on the very first lick, I hit the wire instead and broke it. My father-in-law said he didn't think I was very handy with a hammer either, but he was just kidding me. We'd learned to get along pretty well by then.

Here we are as a newly married couple on the road with the survey team

Jean and I spent our first winter together in Texas, and then traveled back up north in the summer. That was the pattern for the most part: spend the summers surveying northern towns in places like Minnesota and Missouri, and then go south for the winter, to places like Texas, Louisiana, or North Carolina, where it was warm enough to keep working all winter long.

The survey party usually got to avoid wintry weather, but that wasn't always the case. We were in Corrigan, a small town in southern Texas, for the first snow they'd had in years. Some people in town had never seen snow falling before, and they just went crazy with excitement—the little kids especially. The way everyone was acting, I wondered if it was the first time it had *ever* snowed in Corrigan.

Those of us on the survey really didn't have a choice where we went. We'd get our orders to go somewhere, and that's where we went. Most of the time it was in the Midwest because there were other parties that surveyed the coastal states, but once in a while the government would send us out of our usual area.

On the East Coast, we established geodetic controls for mapping projects in the mountains of New Hampshire. We surveyed the Blue Ridge Mountains in Virginia and the mountains in Maryland while stationed in the Virginia towns of Warrenton and Fairfax. In the 1950s, we established geodetic controls for the boundaries of Dulles Airport in Loudoun County, Virginia. It was all just farmland and scrub oak trees back then. Since the airport was put in, the area has become very populated, and Loudoun County has become one of the richest in the United States.

Later in life, after I retired, Jean and I would end up living in Ashburn, Virginia, for a time. It was amazing to see how different the area had become. Ashburn was just a little hole-in-the-wall town when we first went there. You'd drive through without even knowing you went through a town, because there was nothing to see but trees and a few farms. There's hardly anything left now from the time we first went there. An old schoolhouse is still standing, but that's about all there is left of how things used to be.

Our field party took another detour from the Midwest when we traveled to the West Coast to survey the mountains around Crescent, Oregon, as well as nearby Diamond Lake and Crater Lake. That whole area is beautiful. Crater Lake has an island in the middle of it that looks like a ship. We stayed in these old cabins with cracks in the walls that were so big, you could see right through them. That made it pretty cold at times.

I did learn a bit about cooking while I stayed in Oregon. Bunked in the cabin next door was a woman in the survey party who taught me the best way to fry eggs. She showed me how to put a little butter in the skillet and then add the eggs, cooking them just a little before adding some water to steam them. They were so good that I still make eggs this way.

The mountains in Oregon weren't accessible by truck, so we borrowed mules and horses from the U.S. Forest Service to help transport our equipment. The animals were accustomed to working that terrain, because the Forest Service used them all the time to get to the lookout towers where they watched for forest fires. In fact, you could just let go of their reins, and they'd find their way back, all on their own. The animals knew the area better than we did, which was why I should have paid more attention when the one I was riding stopped dead in his tracks and wouldn't move any further.

I tried to force the mule to go up the trail, but he just wouldn't budge. So I got off him and said, "Well, I'll just pull you up this mountain then." I grabbed the reins, but I took no more than two steps when along came a whole swarm of wasps.

I made the mistake of taking off my cap to swat at them. That's when they got in my hair.

I took off running down the trail to try to get away from the wasps. By the time they left me alone, I had been stung all over. Boy, did that hurt. It was so bad, I felt sick to my stomach for a while afterward. I made a vow right then and there: next time, I would listen to the mule.

※

Of all the sixty-some places I lived throughout the country, my favorite was probably the Southwest. I liked New Mexico a lot. The terrain offered a little bit of everything. In a fairly short span, you could drive through mountains, mesas, and plains. I liked the people a lot, too. Because we moved into a town with our own group of friends, we usually got to know local people only when we wanted to go out to eat or have a beer. But New Mexico welcomed us as part of the community by and large, and that has always stuck with me.

The people of Roy, New Mexico, in Harding County—on top of a mesa in the northeastern part of the state—would invite us to functions, like Sunday barbecues in someone's backyard. And I'm not just talking about me and Jean; they'd invite the entire survey party.

There would be weekend barbecues in town as well. The local ranchers would go home on Saturdays and start preparing their barbecues for the party on Sunday. They would make a mesquite fire and cook beef, and then bring it into town. They'd serve it up along with baked beans and the whole works. And they weren't even selling it—it was all free. The local bar owners would sponsor it all to encourage people to come into town to drink.

The whole town of Roy covers an area of only about two square miles. Although only about a thousand people were living there when we arrived (down to just 234 in the 2010 census), Jean and I still made a couple of really good friends. Our closest friends there were two Italian brothers, Bobbie and Roy Regonie, who had grown up in town. We used to laugh about going to visit Roy from Roy. They both got an education at New Mexico University and then came back home to settle down. Bobbie worked in a bank as a vice president, and Roy operated the town bar along with his parents. We used to go to their bar and spend time with them. We liked them so much, we kept in touch after our party moved on, which didn't happen very often with the local people we'd meet. We just met so many going from town to town.

We surveyed the area around Taos, New Mexico, as well. Because it was so mountainous, we had to hike to many of our survey locations. I wasn't a very good hiker. Before I was on the survey, I'd never hiked anyplace in my life. Where I grew up in Kansas, there are some rolling hills, but nothing like what I encountered in places like New Mexico and New Hampshire. By the time I retired, I had hiked a lot of mountains. In New Mexico alone, I hiked a twelve-thousand-foot peak at one time.

In Taos, we hiked in to the survey site with packhorses. The horses carried not only the equipment up the mountain, but most of the survey team as well. I didn't like horses at all, so I usually just walked alongside mine. I like to think I have good reason to dislike them, too. One day we hiked about twelve miles in the mountains before getting back to our trucks. Everyone was tired and just wanted to get home, but those darn horses wouldn't get in the truck. A good friend on the party—Darrell Davis, who was from Osawatomie, Kansas, just north of Topeka—said to me, "Oh, get out of the way, Charlie. I've dealt with horses all my life. I'll get this done." Darrell got in the truck and started pulling on the reins. But instead of those horses cooperating, they lunged right at him. One of them stepped on him, too. For a while after that, I would joke with him about what a great horseman he was. But it just proved my point about horses: they were no good to work with. I was grateful that we only ever had to use them in New Mexico and Oregon.

During one of the last times we were using packhorses in New Mexico, we ran into an electrical storm. It was raining and sleeting so hard, the horses just wouldn't go. They didn't like that storm at all, so we had to coax and push them to the top of the mountain. Once we got there, the situation was even worse: We had no cover. The lightning was striking, and you could smell it—the whole area just stinking with the burnt odor of lightning striking rock. The clouds were hanging too low for us to do the survey. There was nothing to do but wait out the storm.

We ended up spending the whole night on that mountain. It was so cold, and we were all wet. It was a miserable time, I can tell you. All of a sudden, at about five o'clock in the morning, the clouds cleared up and stayed clear long enough to get the job done. We finished the survey, loaded everything back on to the horses, and went back home as quickly as we could.

That's probably my worst memory of my time in New Mexico, but most of the others are good ones, like the time Jean went shopping with a friend in Albuquerque. On the way home, they stopped along the road and picked up several small turtles, thinking the kids in the survey party would enjoy playing with them. When they got back, though, the kids weren't interested at all. I still remember taking those turtles and turning them out on the mesa so they could survive. I didn't mind. Jean always meant well, but after that, I kidded her about the work I sometimes had to do to make up for her good intentions.

Some of my worst experiences on the survey party had to do with losing friends. Everett Daily is someone I will always remember for having the damnedest breath, among other things. One winter, when the survey party was in Knob Noster, Missouri, somebody got sick, so I took the guy's place doing observations that night. Everett went out with me to record, and on our way to the site, he said, "Stop at the gas station. I want to buy some cigars." So we did, and he lit one up as we were driving. He was just smoking and smiling. He seemed like the happiest guy that night.

When we got to the site, just outside Knob Noster, it was really cold. I wanted to get the job done as fast as possible, so I hopped out to look over the site while Everett stayed in the truck to finish his cigar. Pretty soon, I hollered out to him, "Bring those lights out here. Let's set them up. I'm ready to go."

Well, I never got a response. So I hollered again. No response. Finally, I went back to check what was holding things up. There was Everett in the truck, just dead as can be.

Everett's son-in-law worked on the survey, too, and he was on a site about two miles down the road. So I went to get him, and explained that Everett must've had a heart attack. Together, we went to find the coroner, because state law said that we couldn't take the body until after the coroner had come out.

All the while, I kept thinking two things: First, that I wasn't even supposed to be there that night. I was just covering for someone. And second, that Everett had been so happy. I guess you never know when your time is up. You just never expect something like that to happen.

In fact, the same thing happened to me twice. This time it was Joe Benge, the little Frenchman from New Orleans who got me started working on the night crew in the first place.

One night while Joe and I were out working together in Fairfax, Virginia, he kept saying how cold he was. I thought that was a little strange, but otherwise he seemed alright, so I didn't give it too much thought.

After we finished, we came back to our trailer park. Jean had just baked a cherry pie—one of her specialties. So we invited Joe and Thelma in to share some. It was late, probably around eleven p.m., so they had their pie and coffee and then went home, just like it was any other night.

We were getting ready to settle in when we heard a knock at the door. It was Thelma, yelling, "Joe's had a heart attack! Come quick!"

Well, we ran right over, but he was already dead as a mackerel.

Everett and Joe are the only people who ever died on me. Both men suffered heart attacks—although sometimes I kid Jean about Joe, saying that I wonder if it might have been her pie that did him in.

The first time I said that to her, she looked back at me and said, "I was wondering the very same thing."

⁂

When we had Joe and Thelma over for pie that time, we were living in our very first trailer. After living in boarding houses and motels for a while, Jean and I finally got that trailer about a year after we got married.

We had to buy our own trailer on the market—the government didn't buy it for us. As my employer, they gave us per diem to live on, and it was up to us how we spent it. We saved our per diem to purchase our first trailer, knowing we would want some more space and privacy someday, when we were ready to start a family of our own.

Living in the trailer made the survey crew feel even more like a family. When we'd set up at a new site, the trailers that we lived in were placed away from the working trucks and trailers. Everything was close enough that you could walk, but it wasn't like we lived right where we worked. And our neighbors and friends were right next to us. The trailers were all lined up in a row, about ten feet apart because of the fire codes, but probably not any farther than that. It was like living on our own little compound.

In those early years, that trailer was about all Jean and I had. There was no reason to have a car; we used government trucks to pull the trailers from place to place. When we wanted to go for groceries or something, we could take one of the survey trucks into town for that, too. The government didn't mind, so long as we didn't abuse it by using an official vehicle to go to the bar or anything like that.

For those of us who didn't have a car, somebody in the party would let us borrow one when necessary. That's why I didn't get my first car until I was in my midtwenties. It was a used 1957 Chevrolet, and I bought it from a dealer in Oberlin, Kansas. My good friend in the survey party was a mechanic, so we took it apart, ground the valves, and put it back together. The Chevy worked real good after that.

Nobody had credit cards back then, and people hardly wrote checks. Practically all business was done in cash. The only thing we ever bought on credit was that first car. I went to the bank and talked to the president, asking if he would approve a loan for me. I told him how much I was looking to spend—at that time, eight hundred or a thousand dollars would be plenty.

"Sure, Charles," he said. "Go ahead."

So I went out and bought the '57 Chevy.

A week or so later, when I went back to the bank to fill out the paperwork, the president chewed me out royally for writing a check without telling him. We'd already discussed it, so I'd figured that was enough. But he didn't like that I hadn't called him as soon as I'd bought the car. The check I'd written had come into the bank before I had signed any paperwork or even let him know to expect it.

The bank president covered the check anyway, and it didn't take long to pay off the car. I hadn't borrowed that much, so we were settled up within a year. But I still had to listen to that guy lecture me.

"You're going to learn a lesson or two from me," he said. And I suppose I did. After all, that was the last time I bought anything before I had the cash to pay for it. If Jean and I didn't have the money for something, we didn't buy it—it was as simple as that.

Maybe people today should consider taking the same approach.

~~ॐ~~

After New Mexico, Minnesota stands out as a place I liked a lot. Our field party surveyed the western part of the state, including the towns of Litch-field and Crookston, all within a few hours of each other. Once again, it was mostly about the people. Overall, I just liked the people up north. They seemed like really nice, family-oriented folks.

Because our party was landing in a new town every month or so, I developed my ability to size people up very quickly. I had started learning how to do that when I was young, thanks to all the jobs I had along Main Street in Haddam, but I really sharpened those skills with the survey. I spent years on the road, and met so many different people along the way. It got so I could walk into a room and know right off the bat whether I was going to like or dislike a fella. It just comes naturally to me now.

With all the traveling I did, it got so I could strike up a conversation with just about anyone, anywhere. I discovered that most people are pretty receptive if you just start things off. I usually begin by asking where someone is from, and then the conversation goes from there. If you're traveling, that works just about anywhere you are.

When I was working in Crookston, Jean and I decided to go exploring one evening. We went to Grand Forks, North Dakota, which wasn't too far away, and happened into a hotel that had a piano bar. We sat and listened to music for a while, and pretty soon we were singing along. Everyone else was singing, too. Then we struck up a conversation with another couple at the bar. It wasn't long before they were inviting us to the local Elks Club with them. So we went and had dinner with them, danced a little bit afterward, and just had a grand time. The people in Minnesota were just so nice to be around.

Jean and I made friends with a couple in Shelby, Ohio, in a similar way—just struck up a conversation, and pretty soon we were invited over to their house for dinner. They had us over for steaks a few times after that, and I never will forget how the husband cooked them: he charcoaled those steaks. He had this grill with charcoal in the center, and you'd put two steaks in, standing up. I'd never seen anyone cook that way before, but that's how he did it. And boy, those steaks were delicious.

I always remember that couple from Ohio, because they were a reminder to me that people everywhere do things a little differently.

<hr />

After Jean and I had been married for a couple of years, the survey office sent out a letter to all the parties working across the country, asking for volunteers to go work in Alaska. The idea was to survey various sites in that faraway territory, but it wouldn't be the same kind of survey party that I was used to. For one thing, no one was allowed to bring their wives or kids. For another, you would be staying out there for several months, with only occasional letters and packages—no visits—to connect you back home.

There was an upside: it paid more. Plus, it wouldn't cost anything to live. The sites we'd be surveying were out in the middle of nowhere, with no stores to go to, so the government would provide just about everything we needed. At the same time, they were offering extra per diem. That meant I'd be able to save practically all that money.

That didn't happen too often. The per diem we got most places didn't go very far. It was just enough to cover the basics. The survey team was always very conservative, and projects never went over budget. If we got somewhere and there were complications, we just had to make it work. If the money ran out on a project, we just moved to another project that was funded. Sometimes, we might have to go back and finish that project later, but not very often. The government had a timeline for everything, and they knew just about how long it should all take. They knew we typically could finish a project within two weeks, so they'd allow just enough time to finish and get to the next job. You pretty much had to run on schedule—there wasn't any other choice.

That meant there weren't a lot of opportunities to make extra money, so what they were offering for Alaska sounded pretty good. Besides that, I was interested in the experience. I wanted to see what Alaska was like—to do something different and to go explore a different part of the world.

Jean and I talked it over. Spending four months apart, even as newly-weds, sounded okay to her. It was just life. You have to make a living, you know? So I volunteered.

It was early summer of 1951 when I headed off to Alaska. Jean went to stay with her sister, Joanne, in Kansas City, Missouri. She got a job working in the bookkeeping department of the Borden Ice Cream Company. Of course, she didn't tell them she was only going to be staying in Kansas City for the summer. Then again, they didn't ask her if she planned to stick around.

I took a train from Oberlin Park, Kansas, all the way to Seattle. The government paid my way, and the train was an experience in and of itself. I got to see a good part of the country from the window of that train. It was about a two-and-a-half-day journey, traveling both day and night. We stopped along the way for a little bit here and there, so we could get out and stretch our legs, maybe get something to eat. The stop I remember best was Salt Lake City, Utah. I didn't get to see much of it, but I thought it looked like a pretty nice city. All in all, I liked that train ride.

From Seattle, I caught a commercial plane to Anchorage and then a contracted plane to Nunivak Island, where we would be surveying that summer. Jean and I were both in our early twenties then, and it would be our first time apart since we had gotten married two and a half years earlier. Little did we know, this would be just the first of several long-term separations as I surveyed the wilds of Alaska.

A Short History of Nunivak Island
60° 05' 42" N, 166° 12' 40" W

LOCATED IN THE BERING SEA, about thirty miles off the coast of mainland Alaska, Nunivak Island is a permafrost-covered volcanic island. The village of Mekoryuk, located on the north shore, is the island's only permanent settlement, with a population of about two hundred residents. The rest of the island is wilderness.

The inhabitants of Nunivak Island are mostly Cup'ik Eskimos. Famed photographer Edward S. Curtis took a series of photographs of the local people in the 1920s, showing scenes of fishing, kayaking, and other aspects of daily life.

The Yukon Delta National Wildlife Refuge, the second-largest national wildlife refuge in the United States, includes Nunivak Island as part of its territory. The refuge conserves a wide array of shorebirds, seabirds, whistling swans, Canada geese, and marine mammals. Most notable of the island's wildlife may be its herd of musk ox, which were introduced from Greenland in 1935 after the local Alaskan musk ox became extinct. They have been used as breeding stock to reestablish herds elsewhere throughout the region and can be seen wandering about many parts of the 1,700-square-foot island.

Separations and Far-Flung Places

MY FIRST TRIP TO ALASKA WAS to Nunivak Island, which is located in the Bering Sea, between mainland Alaska to the west and Russia to the east. I was sent there in 1951 along with a group of other volunteers from the Coast and Geodetic Survey to do triangulation surveys around the island.

Nunivak had only a couple hundred people living on it, all native Eskimos, so there wasn't exactly an airport. We got to the island by floatplane, traveling across the Etolin Strait. We landed on the sea, right off the coast, even though the water was ice cold. The first thing I saw was a line of Eskimo children wading out into the water to help us carry our gear. Some of them were little kids, too. That cold water didn't bother them at all.

Those Eskimo kids weren't like any little kids that I had ever known. For one thing, they smoked cigarettes. Everybody was smoking cigarettes on the island. For another thing, they liked to take our stuff. They'd come into where we were camped, grab any cigarettes they saw laying around, and just run away. It was pretty unusual, but we didn't care. We could buy cigarettes tax-free—about five cents a pack—on the National Oceanic and Atmospheric Administration (NOAA) ship *Pathfinder*, which was doing a hydrographic survey in the area at the same time.

Something else was unusual about those kids (in my book, at least): their smell. As I found out later, it was from all the blubber they ate.

Nunivak Island is about forty miles wide by sixty miles long, with a mountain in the center of it, called Mount Roberts. When our survey party first arrived, we set up our main camp in the north, in the island's only village: Mekoryuk. That's where most of the Eskimos lived, though there was hardly anything there but homes and a few other buildings.

About twenty-five of us went to Nunivak that year to survey the island. All of us had come from different places and different survey parties around the country, so no one knew each other when we arrived. After a short time at basecamp, we went off in different directions from Mekoryuk in groups of twos—an observer and a recorder.

Once we left the main camp for our surveying assignments, we were out in the middle of nowhere. I didn't see anybody for a good while, except the recorder who was working for me and the pilots who delivered food and took us to new locations. That never did bother me though. I didn't mind the solitude.

What I did mind was that my recorder, Jimmy Cox, didn't have the best hygiene. We had no choice over who we were paired with—each observer was assigned a recorder to work with. Jimmy was from Alamogordo, New Mexico, and he was a good worker, but that's about all I could say for him. When Jimmy and I got to our site, we set up the nine-foot-by-nine-foot tent that would be our home while we were there. We slept on cots and cooked on a Coleman stove fueled with Blazo cans. But I wouldn't let Jimmy cook or do any dishes. I wouldn't let him touch anything like that, because I never did see him wash. Despite that, we got along alright. We kept pretty close quarters with each other all summer, so we had to.

At the beginning of the season, the survey team ordered all the supplies we needed, and they were shipped to the island on the NOAA ship *Pathfinder*. We didn't have an accountant for this project, because we never had to buy anything. There was nowhere to shop anyway. The government sent us all our equipment and supplies: theodolites, tents, cots, and the sleeping bags we used to keep warm. (It was summertime, but it could still get pretty cold.) The wooden stands we put our theodolites on were premade in Seattle and sent up to us already assembled. When we went out to survey a location, usually, the pilots would just bomb our supplies out of an airplane. They attempted to drop the packs somewhere near the site, so when we got there, we had to hunt for our bundle. We always found it, but sometimes it was quite a ways away, and we'd have to haul it all back to camp.

The field party had purchased a food supply in Seattle beforehand, which was enough to last the summer. That was then shipped to Anchorage on the *Pathfinder*, where it was sorted and sent to the survey projects by contracted airplanes. By necessity, our food supply was mostly made up of dried and canned goods. We had things like canned Argentine beef, canned ham, canned vegetables, and ingredients to make pancakes.

I made and ate a lot of pancakes that summer. My family has always loved my pancakes, especially at Christmastime, and I think it's because I really honed my pancake-making skills that summer. I use the basic Betty Crocker recipe from the back of the pancake mix box, but with a bit of a twist. The trick is to thin out the batter with milk until it's the right consistency, and then fry the pancakes. You don't want the batter to be too thick, or you'll get fluffy pancakes. In my family, we like them hard and thin, not fluffy like you get in most restaurants.

There wasn't much variety to what Jimmy and I ate. Sometimes we were sent a slab of bacon, rind and all, which was a treat. At one point, we got a whole ham. Those items lasted a while and wouldn't spoil even though they were unrefrigerated, because it never did get hot on that island.

We couldn't really hunt or fish, because everything on the island was wormy. Besides that, the Eskimos made the rules around there, and we were prohibited from having guns. The Eskimos were allowed to hunt, though. On the island, they had about five thousand reindeer and some seventy-five head of musk ox. During the summer months, the whole tribe would go out and herd all these reindeer into a corral that they had built on one end of the island. Then they castrated a lot of them, and killed some others to eat or send over to the mainland to sell. They'd keep the best males and females for the next go around.

I remember waking up one morning in August to find three musk ox right outside our little tent. Jimmy and I had set up camp by a lake, and the musk ox were out there by the water, just rutting and rutting. We had been warned to stay out of their way. They could charge at any time during the mating season, so I kept my distance.

I was able to get pretty close to this little silver fox one time. I had a little food, which I held right up to his nose. He didn't seem scared of me, but he wouldn't take the food either—not until I dropped it. Then he took the food, and ate it right up. That was pretty neat to see.

⁂

Our party had been sent out to survey the area around Mount Roberts, and then the job would be done. The problem on Nunivak Island was the weather: it was the pits. At one point, we got stuck at a location for twenty-six days. With all the rain and fog, we couldn't see the top of the mountain, so we couldn't work. Because the visibility was so bad, a plane couldn't get in to fly us out of the area either. So the pilots had to fly overhead and drop us some food to get us through. I ate only canned carrots and lima beans for two or three days, because that's all we had left. By the time they were finally able to drop more food, I was pretty tired of carrots and lima beans.

Another time, Jimmy and I had set out across the tundra to survey an area that was about an hour's walk from the tent. We got to the site and started working. All of a sudden, the fog came rolling in. The fog moved pretty quick on the island, so we weren't always prepared for it.

Jimmy and I had to get back to the tent somehow, but we could hardly see a thing. The terrain we had walked across was as flat as could be, so there were no markers—no trees or hills or anything—to help us find our way. The only thing I could think to do was take out my compass. On the way there, I had taken a compass reading probably halfway between our camp and the worksite. So I aimed the compass at that bearing, and we starting walking.

Every once in a while, I would check the compass to make sure we were still heading in the right direction. There was no way to tell for sure, but I did my best. We walked a long time, just hoping we weren't veering off in the wrong direction.

We had pitched our tent near a lake so we would have access to water. There were always two or three loons on that lake, and I had taken to watching them during our time there. After we'd been walking a good while, I heard the squawking of those loons. That's when I knew for sure that we were on the right track. We still couldn't see more than an arm's length ahead of us, however, so we just kept walking. All of a sudden, there in front of us was the opening to our tent.

I was shocked. It was like a mirage appearing out of the fog. But it was real, and I couldn't have been more relieved. In fog that thick, it would have been easy to walk right by camp and wander off into the tundra. But instead, with just my compass, I had managed to guide us not only back to camp, but right back to our front door!

Another time that summer, the crew of the *Pathfinder*, which was doing a hydrographic survey, needed some help to put in a tide gauge. So my boss said to me, "You can take the ship to your next point. They'll drop you off, and you can help put in a tide gauge." He thought that was a pretty good idea. Taking the ship rather than being flown there would save some money.

When I agreed to that, I had no idea what I was in for.

When the *Pathfinder* came to pick me up, one of the officers took a launch and beached it on a sandbar. I went out in a whaleboat to meet it, along with the other junior officer. When we got there, we couldn't get that launch off the sandbar. A huge boulder right beside us was threatening to beat the bottom out of it. If those officers let that happen, they would have really caught hell.

So I was out there in this whaleboat, getting wet and cold, as they tried to pull the launch off the sandbar without damaging the boat. It didn't work, so finally they gave up. Another launch had to come pick us up to take us to the ship.

We got to the *Pathfinder* in the end, but my troubles weren't over. The only way up the side of this big ship was to grab hold of a rope ladder hanging down its side. You're in the launch alongside the ship, and when the wave lifts you up, you're supposed to grab that rope ladder and just shimmy up as fast as you can, so the next guy behind you can grab on to it. I didn't like that idea too much. You had to have pretty good timing to make it work.

I told the officer that I would rather ride the launch back up to the boat. After all, they were going to be putting a wench on the launch and hauling it back aboard the ship. I figured I could just get a ride up that way. But the officer said no, that was against regulation. I had to get up that ladder.

I managed to climb it, but I wasn't too happy about it. The only good thing about being aboard that ship was that, after the whole episode, Captain Robert Earl had me and the junior officers into his office for a shot of whiskey. Alcohol wasn't allowed on Nunivak Island, so I hadn't had a drink the whole time I was there. After being out there in the cold water for so long, I sure needed one.

That was the last good thing that happened to me on that ship. It was rough water, and I started to feel seasick. I walked by the kitchen where there was food cooking, and that was all it took. I was sick for the next three days.

The last job I did after leaving Nunivak Island was the hardest. We were surveying a point on the top of Black Mountain that was pretty inaccessible, so Jimmy and I had to hike up to it. Getting there took about two and a half hours, with each of us carrying about fifty pounds. We had to haul our tent, the theodolite and stand, the lights, and all our food and supplies. It was a lot to carry and a long way to carry it.

I wasn't used to hiking mountains, so I wasn't in the best shape for it. At most sites I'd surveyed, the only thing I'd had to climb was the tower. Let me tell you, that was a lot easier than hiking with a fifty-pound pack—especially through the tundra of Alaska. We always seemed to be making our way through water or across these little mounds on the tundra, which made for very rough walking.

Meanwhile, back home, Jean didn't know a thing about what my Alaskan experience was like. Letters took forever to get to the States, so there were long stretches between our communications. At least when she didn't hear from me for a while, she had no idea that she might need to worry about me being stranded somewhere and running out of food.

We did try to keep in touch, even though the mail service was unreliable. At one point, Jean even made me cookies and sent them by regular mail to Alaska, not realizing just how long that would take. I never did get those cookies. Maybe somebody along the way enjoyed them instead.

When my first summer in Alaska came to a close, I wasn't sorry to be done with it. I came out of the experience with a lot of extra money, but that didn't make me want to stay. I had been on Nunivak for more than three months, and I was happy to be leaving it behind.

To get home, all the other people in the survey party rode back to Seattle on the *Pathfinder*. But I didn't get the ship ride back. Somebody was needed to do one last job on the mainland, and that somebody ended up being me. I finished up that job as quickly as I could, and then finally got to head home.

I flew into Kansas City to meet Jean in the fall of 1951, right after the city was hit by a big flood. As the airplane began its descent into the city, I looked out the window and saw what looked like a disaster area. The rising waters had deposited mud all over the place and left a real mess. Neither of us had known what the other had been through while we were apart.

The airport was on a plateau in an area of the city that had taken the worst of it. Thankfully, Jean worked in a part of the city that was on higher ground, so the aftermath wasn't so bad where she was. Needless to say, Jean and I had a pretty good reunion.

⁂

The Korean War had started in 1950, and by the time I returned from Alaska, guys were already being drafted into the fight. I was the right age to be drafted, and others on the survey were getting called up. But I didn't have to go, and for a very good reason: Jean got pregnant. That got me out of my first notice. I never did hear from the draft board again.

Our first child, David, was born in October 1952 in a small hospital in Beeville, Texas, which was where we were working that fall. It was an easy birth, and I was there when he was born. Jean got to stay in the hospital for eight days while the nurses took care of her and David. They won't do that for you now unless you have medical difficulties, but back then it was pretty common.

We brought David home to the trailer, and all and all, I think we adjusted to being parents pretty quickly. We didn't go out as much. We took our responsibilities more seriously. My sister, Donna, lived in a trailer nearby—her husband, Bill Perkins, had started working on the survey, too—so she was around to help Jean out. Donna already had a little baby of her own, so she knew the ropes.

My niece Patty was barely a year old the first time she came over with her mother to visit her newborn cousin. Jean had laid David on the couch. Everyone was cooing and carrying on over him, when that little gal came over and bit the baby's finger. David started crying, and poor Donna was so upset. But that was about the worst of it, and otherwise things were going smoothly—until I got the notice that I was being sent to Alaska again the following summer.

Life changed after David was born. I'd had enough of Alaska after my trip the previous summer, so I really didn't want to go back. And now I had this new baby boy. . . . But this time, they didn't ask for volunteers. Instead, they assigned my whole survey party to go, whether we liked it or not. Once again, it was just workers—no families—so I would have to leave Jean again for several months, this time with a new baby to take care of.

I left in May, when David was not yet seven months old. This time, Jean traveled home to Missouri with the baby so she'd have her parents around to help her while I was gone.

On my second trip to Alaska, the whole survey party was sent to work in McKinley National Park, which is now known as Denali National Park. This time my brother-in-law, Bill, was assigned to work as my recorder. We didn't get along very well, possibly because he thought he should have my job. So there was some friction there—nothing I couldn't handle, but it ended up being a long summer.

One time, Bill and I shot two caribou with a gun I had won in a poker game. We butchered and processed the hindquarters, then packed the meat up the mountain and placed it in a snowbank to preserve it. That was the only thing I ever shot in Alaska, because we didn't typically have guns there. I sold mine later on, because I didn't want to carry it back with me. Come to find out, that park was full of bears. But the government never did warn us of any danger, and they certainly didn't supply us with any guns to protect ourselves. Anyway, the meat was so bad, even the bears wouldn't eat it.

Years later, after I retired, Jean and I took a trip to Denali Park while we were on a cruise to Alaska. One of the highlights of that trip was meeting Barbara and Truman Dehner, from Morehead, Kentucky. We enjoyed their company very much and would have our nightly cocktails and dinner on the cruise ship together. I remember telling them how much the place had changed. It wasn't nearly as remote as when I'd worked there. There's a hotel now and a number of other buildings where there was absolutely nothing before. One thing hadn't changed though: nobody had ever been killed by a grizzly bear in the park, according to our guide. But that was then. Soon after we returned home, we heard a story on the news about somebody wandering off the trail and being mauled by a grizzly—the first person known to be killed by one in Denali National Park. I couldn't help but think about all the far-out, isolated terrain I had hiked years earlier. When I was working there, I never did get close to a bear, but a black bear got into one guy's tent and tore everything up, looking for food. That bear didn't hurt anyone—no one was in the tent at the time—but he sure did make a mess.

We surveyed some pretty remote locations in Denali National Park. Getting there required a different setup than we'd had on Nunivak. Helicopters would take us to the worksite somewhere, along with our supplies, equipment, and food all packed up in boxes on the skids of the 'copter, one on each side. We'd load up those boxes with everything we needed before we took off; then we'd unload them once we landed at our location. Sometimes, if we had loaded them down too much, the helicopter would try to take off, but then immediately set back down so the pilot could lighten the load. We took two-seater Piper Cub airplanes to certain locations, and it was the same setup. We needed a lot of equipment for the work we were doing, and it added up to a lot of weight.

Once we got somewhere and unloaded the boxes, the 'copter or plane would fly off and leave us there with only radios and Morse code to communicate any problems with basecamp. After that, our tent was our salvation. When the weather wasn't good, there was little to do but hunker down in the tent and wait. I read a lot. Bill and I had a radio at one point, but the reception was so bad that we couldn't do much with it. For some reason, we didn't even play cards. Once in a while, we would chat a bit, but we didn't even do that all that much.

At one station in the park, the wind was blowing so bad that we couldn't keep the tent up. We were set up alongside a large boulder, and the wind cut right through the ropes that held up the tent. We built a rock wall around the tent to protect it from the wind, but that wasn't enough. The tent got all torn up. We finally had to abandon it and go back to basecamp. That tent is probably still out there somewhere.

When my brother-in-law and I had a bit of spare time in between jobs, we went down to visit a family that was living in an old mining area that we had passed through. They had bought the land around this abandoned mine and now spent their summers looking for gold, using a sifter. Their goal was to take twenty thousand dollars worth of gold out of there each year for twenty years. They let us sift through some extra barrels of dirt that they had taken out the season before, looking for little bits of gold. There wasn't much to do in our spare time, so we were happy to do it. We did find a few nuggets, but I gave them to my brother-in-law. I don't remember why exactly. I should have kept them.

Another time when we were in between projects, we played a joke on this guy in our party. His name was Carl Orlup, and he was a strange guy. One day, he got it in his head that he really wanted a chicken to eat. I guess he'd gotten tired of eating the same old food. Of course, there aren't a lot of chickens running around the Alaskan wilderness—but there were a lot of loons. So a couple of guys shot a loon and skinned it. The meat was bright white, kind of like fish—all loons eat is fish, so I guess that's why. Those guys dropped off that meat for Carl and told him it was his chicken. I don't know if he ate it, but I imagine he wasn't too happy about the joke.

Up in Alaska during the summertime, it's daylight most of the time. Sometimes you couldn't work very long hours, because you needed darkness to really get the job done. We got there in the late spring as the days were lengthening, but by the time we left in October, it was getting dark earlier. And boy, would it get dark there at night. You could hardly see a thing.

Late in the season, we got snowed in for a time near Wonder Lake. We were at the end of the road that runs through the park, and it had gotten so packed with snow that there was no way to drive out. Helicopters picked us up to take us out of there, so we had to leave the trucks and things behind. We took our theodolite with us, though—we couldn't leave that behind—so I had to sit there in the helicopter with the instrument between my legs.

While we were flying back to basecamp in this 'copter with the pilot and his wife, the throttle froze. I guess that happens at around five thousand feet when it's so cold out. So we had to fly into the airstrip at McKinley Park and do a dead-stick landing. The rotor was still going, but nothing else was working. The pilot couldn't maneuver at all. We had to glide in, with the pilot pointing the aircraft in the right direction and hoping for the best. We hit the ground—*bang!*—and skidded about seventy-five feet. As soon as the helicopter stopped moving, I opened the door and jumped out. I didn't want to be in it one second longer.

In the park, there were these openings in the canyon where the wind could become really fierce. We lost a pilot and one of our junior officers that way. They were flying in a Piper Cub and were running a little too low. They got caught in one of those wind tunnels. It just slapped the plane right to the ground and killed them. Mount Scott was named after the junior officer who died in that crash.

That was a problem with these trips: some of the pilots weren't too experienced. The Coast Survey brought in guys from all over the country, and most of them didn't know the terrain or have any experience with how quickly the wind could shift or the fog could role in. It could get pretty dicey at times.

By the time we had finished the job, I was more than ready to go home once again. David was just a baby when I left. By the time I returned, he was almost a year old and running around. We had our reunion on the West Coast. Jean had driven her parents out to California to see one of her sisters who was living there. Then she and David drove up to meet me in Klamath Falls, Oregon, where I'd been assigned to a small job on my way back.

When I first saw them, David came running right up, just like I had never gone away. Maybe he remembered me, or maybe Jean and her parents had been telling him about me. Either way, he sure was glad to see me. I never will forget that.

Jean and baby David greet me at the trailer

The following year, in the summer of 1953, it happened again: the government sent our entire crew to Alaska for the season. Once again, we didn't have a choice.

Instead of taking a train out west this time, I rode with a friend of mine who was going to Alaska too. The car carried four of us from the survey party: me, Alvin Woods, and two other guys. On our way up north, we stopped in Bend, Oregon, where Alvin's parents lived—the nicest people I'd ever met. We spent the night there.

There wasn't much to Bend, as I recall, but we had this mess of smelt for dinner that had come from the nearby Columbia River. Somebody also left a huge piece of venison on the porch, which Alvin's mom roasted. I don't like venison, but the smelt was so good. And we were really happy to have that last home-cooked meal, since the eating options were pretty limited up in Alaska.

When we got to Alaska, we started work in Denali National Park so we could finish up the job we had started the year before. We also worked around the Wrangell Mountains, which was really out in the boondocks, and in Copper Center, Chitina, Bethel, and Hooper Bay.

In Copper Center, we camped at an airstrip near some copper mines. The place had been abandoned as a result of copper becoming so cheap; it looked just like a ghost town. There were these buildings attached to the airstrip, houses that people had once lived in. Everything in them was as neat as a pin. It looked like the people who lived there had disappeared all of a sudden, leaving everything behind. It was like going back in time.

Alvin was my recorder on that third trip to Alaska. He was a fun guy to be with all summer, because you never knew what he was going to do. When we first got to Copper Center, we started off by looking for water, as we did in every new place we went to. You have to have water to survive, so that was always the first thing we did to get situated.

But little Alvin liked to drink. As we had flown into Cooper Center, Alvin had been in the back of the plane, drinking whiskey. He was pretty inebriated by the time we arrived, but we still had some things we needed to get done. When we landed, I told him to go looking for water at one end of the airport, and I'd check in the opposite direction.

I walked no more than half a mile before I found a fresh stream, so I turned around and went back to where we were going to pitch a tent. We still had to get the camp set up, but now I couldn't find Alvin. Walking in the direction I'd sent him, I came across a little cabin. I opened the door . . . and there was Little Alvin. Instead of looking for water, he'd gone into that cabin and fallen asleep.

When I woke him up, he jumped to his feet and started swinging at me.

I just threw him down on the floor—he was a small man, and a little out of it, so it wasn't too hard—and then I told him he better get his act together. And he did. Alvin wasn't a bad guy. He'd just been startled when I woke him up is all. We had a good laugh about it later.

Another reason Alvin was a good guy to be paired with was his cooking. He was a really good cook. He'd bake things out in the wild, which wasn't easy. He made an oven out of a Blazo can and baked pies using dried goods and canned fruit. We sometimes had fresh fruit, too, when we picked it ourselves. The wild blackberries and raspberries were really good. That's what the bears ate most of the time. They really loved those berries.

Once, about halfway through the season, when we returned for a brief stint to basecamp near the Wrangell Mountains, Little Alvin decided that he wanted to eat some fresh meat. He went out hunting with one of the helicopter pilots, and the two of them shot a couple of dall sheep from the side of the 'copter. By the time the pilot was able to circle back to the spot, only one sheep was left—bears probably got the other. Anyway, Alvin and the pilot brought that sheep back and cooked it up. It was really tasty. The whole party was at basecamp then, so it didn't last long, which was too bad. I think it was probably the best meat I've ever had.

Dall sheep have these big, curved horns, and Alvin got it into his head that he wanted to take those horns back to Bend as a memento. He lugged those things around in a sack for the rest of summer. They were heavy, but he wouldn't leave them behind. He had his heart set on bringing them home.

Because there wasn't much variety, we often got tired of what we had to eat. If we got a chance to have something different, we usually took it. In Bethel, there was a roadhouse where you could get something to eat, so we'd go when we could. It was next to a river, which would ice over in the winter. Guys at the roadhouse liked to place bets on when it would get warm enough for the ice on that river to start moving again. That was a big thing in Alaska—betting on the ice flow. As for me, if I started to get excited about sitting around, waiting for ice to melt, I'd take it as a sign that I'd been in Alaska too long.

After that third trip, our entire party was never assigned to go back again. I could have volunteered, but I really didn't want to go back. I'd had my adventure in Alaska, and by then I was ready for something different.

A Short History of King Ranch, Texas
27° 30' 54" N, 97° 51' 56" W

NAMED AFTER RICHARD KING, a New York steamboat captain, King Ranch occupies a sprawling stretch of land in southwest Texas, about forty miles from Corpus Christi. King first came to the area to serve in the Mexican–American war under General Zachary Taylor, who later became the nation's twelfth president. After the war, King was inspired to stay; and in 1853, he and a partner bought the first tract of land that would become his famed ranch.

King continued to acquire land throughout his life, using it as grazing land for a variety of animals, most notably cattle and horses. Through the years, King Ranch has also been used for farming and for the production of oil and gas. In addition, it is home to a wide array of wildlife including deer, quail, wild hog, wild turkeys, antelope, giant rattlesnakes, and more.

After King's death, his heirs continued the business, and now King Ranch is the largest ranch in the country. It spans approximately 825,000 acres across six counties in southern Texas. It was designated a National Historic Landmark in 1961 and now includes a museum and a visitor center, attracting both tourists and hunters.

Bugs, Snakes, and Other Scary Experiences

WHEN YOU'RE YOUNG, EVERYTHING IS A new deal, a new experience. You don't get scared all that often, because you don't know any different. Whatever happens, you usually just go with it. That was especially true on the survey. We were always showing up in new places where there were new people, new things to see, new problems to solve.

Looking back, I realize I had some pretty unusual experiences, even some dangerous ones. I just didn't think about it like that at the time. I was working so much, I didn't really have a chance to stop and ponder such things.

Take the bugs, for example. When I was a kid in Haddam, I was pretty scared of that swarm of grasshoppers that came in like a giant storm cloud and took over my grandparents' farm. But on the survey, encounters with bugs and other unpleasant things became a somewhat regular way of life.

In Alaska, because the survey party was there in the summertime, the weather was cold but not completely freezing. You had to dig down about twelve inches to hit permafrost. That meant it was a perfect environment for mosquitoes. You could be someplace working, and it would be just a nice, clear day. Then all of a sudden, just like with those grasshoppers, a cloud of mosquitos would appear out of nowhere—so many of them, you'd get to choking on the dang things. And boy, would they bite you all over.

We slept with mosquito nets over our cots, but they still managed to get inside. There were just too many of them. We couldn't keep them out, no matter what we did. I had this pair of jeans that I liked to work in, and one day I doused the legs with mosquito repellent. It gave me a bit of a break from the things, so I wore those jeans all summer long. The mosquitos were worse than the bears in those parts.

Alaska was pretty bad in that way; but when it came to pests, I believe Louisiana came out on top. At one point, I was working in Grand Isle, Louisiana, which is at the southern end of this little neck that stretches out into the Gulf of Mexico. There are all sorts of big hotels and things to do there now, but at the time it was little more than a sand pile surrounded by water.

One night after I'd finished working, I returned to my truck. I was sitting there with the door open when I turned on the dome light to get myself organized. I really wasn't thinking when I did that, because that one little light was enough to attract every mosquito around. Before I had a chance to do anything, hundreds of mosquitos swarmed in and just took over the truck. I'm telling you, we had mosquitos in there for—well, I don't know how long. We had a heck of a time getting rid of them all after that.

Louisiana was not my favorite place to work. The survey team was in Shreveport for a time, up in the northwestern part of the state and away from the coast—so there weren't so many bugs, but the area had nuisances of a different kind. Shreveport was once home to cotton plantations, though by the time we arrived, it was more of a busy industrial city. Oil was big business, and so was paper. The problem was, the smell and the soot from the paper mills were everywhere. You'd park your car and come back to it a while later, and it would be covered with a layer of grit. If you left it on there for too long, that stuff would eat the paint right off your car.

The best part of working in Louisiana wasn't really in Louisiana at all. It was out in the Gulf of Mexico, off the coast of New Orleans, where we were sent to survey some of the oil platforms.

Because the platforms weren't high enough, the party had to build survey towers on them. So we had to gather everything we needed to build the towers on the mainland, and then haul it out to the platforms by boat. One time, we had a barge loaded with steel when the tide went out, and we were left sitting right in the middle of a mudflat. We couldn't move until the tide came back in. It was a long wait, but it gave me a chance to notice how amazing the ground was there. The muddy Mississippi River washes all sorts of sediment down into the Gulf, creating a base of thick sludge. We could take one of our twelve-foot-long two-by-fours and push it straight down into the muddy ground. It went in easy, like there was no bottom, and it would just stand there, straight up in the air.

Once we got our supplies and equipment out to the platforms, those of us working as observers and recorders would travel back and forth to the mainland by boats furnished by the oil companies. People did a lot of shrimping around that area, so sometimes we'd get some fisherman to take us out too. The problem was, those shrimpers were used to sticking to the channels. The platforms were further out, in open water—as far as one hundred miles offshore. Some of the local fishermen weren't too savvy about traveling out that far. If we hadn't charted their course for them, we would never have gotten there.

Sometimes, after we got set up on the oil platforms, we would stay overnight to work. That was the part of being in Louisiana that I really did like. The oil company served food around the clock—all day and all night—because there were shifts of rig workers going all the time. The drilling never stopped. The rig workers were out there for two weeks at a time. Then they'd go back to shore for a week before going right back out again. It was hard work and an even harder schedule, so the company had to keep its people happy. That must be why it was the best food I had anywhere in the country.

On those oil rigs, you could get whatever you wanted to eat, anytime you wanted it—twenty-four hours a day, seven days a week. Steak. Lobster. Anything, really. It was a first-class operation. I ended up going out to the platforms three or four times, staying two or three days each time. We would sleep in the same quarters as the rig workers, on a big ship tied to the rig. It was nothing much—just a small bunk in a room with everyone else's—but I didn't mind it. The food was that good.

Jean and David stayed on shore while I was out on the rig. One of the places where the survey set up camp was in a town called Galliano, on the Bayou Lafourche, which flows into the Gulf. It wasn't too far from Grand Isle, just a bit north, but still out there near the mainland's southern edge. It's mostly swampland in those parts. A lot of the fishermen went there to clean their fish and shrimp, so an awful smell hung in the air. Even though we were surveying there in the winter, it was still pretty hot, which didn't help the stench. That was tough to take, but that wasn't the worst part about Galliano. Once again, the biggest problem was the darn mosquitos.

The mosquitos were so bad, Jean finally decided she couldn't take it any longer. They really infected her system, so she would get these big welts on her legs after she'd been bit. More than that, she couldn't let David outside to play, because he'd get all bit up too. The two of them were pretty miserable. One morning, she woke up and said, "Charles, I got to get out of here."

We talked about it and decided she should take David to her parents' house in Missouri until I finished the job. Then we'd meet up after I'd moved on to somewhere less buggy.

We had a car by then, but it was going to be quite a drive to Missouri from where we were—through Louisiana, Mississippi, and Arkansas, and it was still mostly just two-lane roads. But Jean was determined. She put little David in the car, and away they went.

Jean spent the first night in a hotel along the road. The next morning, when she was ready to take off again, she spotted a serviceman in uniform, hitchhiking north. She'd seen him more than once the day before, hitching rides along her route, so she decided to give him a ride. Our family teases her now about how dangerous it could've been—picking up a stranger!

with a baby in the car!—but it wasn't such an uncommon thing to do back then, especially for a military man. Besides, it was a long drive and she wanted someone to talk to.

~⁄⁄~

In south Texas, the survey party was assigned to perform geodetic surveys on King Ranch, the largest ranch in the United States, which dates back to 1853. We were way out in the boonies, in what's known as the Wild Horse Desert, so we had to camp out near a roadhouse, which was the only thing around. One day, I woke up and my arm was just as red as a beet. It was the mosquitos again.

Turned out I had flopped my arm outside my mosquito net while I was sleeping, so they had some fresh meat to feast on for a while. I was a little surprised that it didn't wake me up. Then again, I never did have any problems sleeping.

Of course, bugs weren't the only hazard in a place like that. Sometimes, just the remoteness of the locations we surveyed was a problem in itself. I was still camping on King Ranch, in the middle of nowhere, when I got an abscessed tooth. It was so bad, I had to quit working and find a dentist right away. The nearest one was in Raymondville, a town of about ten thousand people located more than an hour away. It was a long drive there, I can tell you. The dentist ended up pulling all four of my wisdom teeth, but I wasn't about to complain. I was really glad to get rid of them, especially the abscessed one.

And then there were the snakes.

In parts of west and central Texas where we worked, like around Abilene, there were small rattlers about. One time, I was opening a gate when I saw one of those little prairie rattlers, so I went and got a shovel. I let that snake strike the shovel over and over again until it finally just wore itself out. Then I was able to get by it and through the gate without any trouble.

When we got into southeast Texas, however, the snakes were something else. The rattlesnakes there were huge, like nothing I'd ever seen before. Our party surveyed two large ranches near Victoria, owned by two separate families that had been rivals for years. At least, that was the rumor we were told. I went to work one day and saw a fence lined with dead snakes— all these enormous diamondback rattlers hanging over it. They were maybe three to four inches in diameter and a full six feet long. The ranch hands would kill them and hang them there. I don't know why.

There was a lot of game on those ranches, too. The Mexicans who camped out on the land back in those days told us that people would fly in on small planes without permission, shoot something, and then take off again before anyone could catch them. The hunting was that good. Maybe the ranch hands hung up those big snakes as some kind of warning against intruders.

Thankfully, I never did get too close to one of the big rattlesnakes in Texas—not one that was alive anyway. But I did get too close for comfort to some snakes in West Virginia.

The party was sent to do a survey in the mountains of West Virginia, at a site that was really out in the sticks. As we hiked in to the survey point, we'd sometimes happen on little shacks where people were living. I don't know what they did to earn a living way out there. There was moonshine around, and maybe a little bit of farming in small patches, though the land was too hilly and rocky for large farms. Anyway, they were out there, so somehow they made it work.

I ran into a guy once in those mountains and asked him for directions. I explained what we were doing there and where we wanted to go. He didn't say a word the entire time I was talking. Then all of a sudden he said, "C'mon, follow me," and he took off. It was all my recorder and I could do to keep up with him as he wound his way through the hills. He never did say another word after that—just led us to our site and then disappeared into the trees.

I was surveying up in the mountains near Elkins, West Virginia, with my recorder, Jim Fuchs, when we had the snake encounter. There were a lot of copperheads in those parts, and you usually knew when they were near. You could smell them. They lived together in dens that gave off this really musty smell. Jim and I were up on a mountain, near a four-foot stand we were using for our theodolite. I was doing the observation, and Jim was sitting on a rock nearby, recording for me. All of a sudden, here comes a copperhead slithering around the edge of the rock he was on. The thing just popped right out of this hole and went right toward Jim.

Jim's eyes opened wide when he saw that copperhead near his feet, and his body froze. He had a real fear of snakes. And then—no joke—all of a sudden, here comes another snake out of the same hole. A rattler this time—it went right past Jim's legs.

I saw the whole thing happen from a couple of feet away, and I thought Jim was going to die of fright right then and there. But Jim never did move, and both snakes went right past him.

West Virginia has lots of snakes. We knew that, and we knew not to walk around in the dark at night in case we might step on one. If we absolutely had to be moving around, we would walk fast and step high with our boots on. But we never figured one would just pop out of a hole, right next to where we were working. We never thought one would do that, so we certainly never figured on two.

While I was in Elkins, I also got myself into a bit of trouble of a different kind. I had some free time, so I went down to the store and bought a crate of chickens, thinking I would give one to every family in the survey party so we could all have a nice dinner. Out at the camp, I started to butcher and clean those chickens. Well, instead of making everybody happy, all the women in camp hated my guts. A lot of them hadn't grown up on farms like Jean and I had, so they weren't used to seeing their dinner get killed before they ate it like we were. I learned my lesson after that.

∼⅊⌇∼

It seemed as if most of our strangest encounters happened in the southern part of the country. Some of these places, like the ranches we surveyed in Texas, paid the government to survey their land. That was what happened with AC Spark Plug, a company located in a remote area of Texas.

When we drove up to the location we'd been given, there was nothing else around. I was wondering why they would have a spark plug company in such an isolated spot. Well, by the time we finished the job, I wasn't so sure it was spark plugs they were making there at all.

Our chief of party assigned a subparty—just a few of us from the main party—to go out to this job. I was in charge, so I took a crew of about five guys with me. When we arrived, there was a big fence around the place. Guards were posted at the entrance, and they wouldn't let us in. I don't know why a spark plug company required so much security, but they had a whole setup there. They told us we had to have security clearance to get on the grounds, but we didn't have it.

Well, we had driven all the way out there, and I wasn't excited about the idea of just turning around and going back without having done a single thing. Remember, we got paid by the project, so it wasn't like we made more if it took us longer to complete. If we turned around and went home, we'd probably have to drive back the next day once the security issue was figured out. It would be much better if they would just let us do our work now. So I decided to raise all kinds of hell.

"Your boss is paying us to do this work," I told the guard. "If you don't let us get started, I'm going to take my crew and leave, and your boss will be paying for nothing." I was bluffing a bit, but the guard did seem worried about getting into trouble.

Finally I got him to assign another guard to stay with us while we worked, to make sure we didn't get into any trouble. But once we got inside the facility, it was the strangest thing: they wanted us to determine geodetic positions on each room in the building. I don't know why. No one had asked for anything like that before, nor did anyone ask it ever again—not while I was working for the survey. But that's what they wanted, so we got to work.

We started establishing coordinates for several rooms in the facility—rooms that were completely empty. We couldn't figure it out. Why did the company need all this information on a bunch of nothing? We asked, but they never did tell us anything—except that there was some sort of scientific project going on there. I later read about how a company called AC Spark Plug built the B-36 bombing navigation system that helped end the Cold War. I wondered if that's what they were working on in that building we surveyed. But I guess I'll never know for sure.

The worst of the bugs, snakes, and strange experiences may have been in the south, but I encountered creepy-crawly things in other places, too. One time, after the survey party had completed a survey in Minnesota, we had a short break before moving to the next location. So Jean and I took David to the lake to go swimming. It was a nice, warm summer day, and he was having a grand old time. That is, until he got out of the lake, and we saw that he had leeches all over him.

We had to pull those leeches off David's skin one by one and throw them back into the water. But he didn't mind that too much—not as much as he minded the sunburn he got that day. We spent the following day in the car, traveling to our next site, and Jean had to put up with some amount of misery from him because he was so uncomfortable. I doubt he remembers those leeches, but he may yet remember that sunburn.

~\|/~

When David was nearly three years old, we found out Jean was pregnant with our second child. I was headed down to Mississippi to work on a new project, but Jean didn't feel like traveling that far. Nor was she thrilled about being somewhere that might be hot and buggy when the baby came. She also sensed that it was going to be tough to manage a newborn and a three-year-old at the same time. So when she was getting near her due date, she decided to go to her parents' house in Meadville for a while.

That's why I wasn't there when Susan was born. I wasn't there for the complications either, which may well have been the scariest thing that happened to us during that time in our lives.

When I got the call from Jean's parents, I was working in Batesville, Mississippi. Nobody in the survey party had a phone of their own back then. If someone wanted to get in touch with you or leave you a message, they had to call the main office trailer. The chief of party had just one phone in the trailer for everybody to use. Jean's parents called that phone, and somebody relayed the message to me out in the field.

I caught a train from Mississippi right away. As distracted as I was, I couldn't help but notice that it had segregated cars—blacks were in one car and whites in another. Where I came from, in Kansas, they didn't have anything like segregated cars. That train took me to Marceline, Missouri, about twenty miles from Meadville and about thirty miles from Chillicothe, where Jean and Susan were in the hospital.

When Jean's parents called to tell me the baby had been born, they didn't tell me about all the problems Jean had dealt with. She had been to see the doctor the same day she had given birth, and he told her everything was fine. In fact, he thought it would be another week before the baby came. So Jean went back to her parents' farm and had a normal enough evening. But then she woke up in the middle of the night because she didn't feel quite right. Her mother heard her get up and came to check on her. That's when she saw all the blood.

"Is this normal?" Jean asked her mother. It hadn't been like that with David, but she still wasn't sure.

"Oh my God, no," her mother said, and she ran to the phone to call an ambulance.

Jean had a ruptured placenta and had to go to the nearest hospital, where she had an emergency cesarean section. I didn't learn about the extent of it until after I arrived. Everything was okay by then, so I never had to worry too much. I just wanted to see Jean and the baby.

David was being looked after by his grandparents. He always liked being on their farm. He used to follow his granddad around while he was working in the farmyard and imitate the things he said. Knowing David was in good hands, I went straight to the hospital first. What a great relief it was when I finally saw my beautiful little baby girl! I held her in my arms and really thought I'd hit the jackpot.

We didn't have insurance back then—a lot of people didn't, even those of us who worked for the government. So despite all she was going through during her delivery, Jean made a point of reassuring the doctor that we had the money to pay him. All he said to her was, "Don't you worry about the money. I'm not worrying about it, so neither should you." It sure isn't like that now. We still think about how well Jean was treated even though the hospital had no guarantee they were going to get paid. And if I remember correctly, the whole thing, C-section and all, cost only $125.

※

The segregated train I took from Mississippi is just one example of the racial tensions we witnessed while we were in the South in the 1950s. It was something we never could get used to.

Walking down the street one time in Batesville, David and I passed a large, strong-looking black man on the street. David was looking closely at him—I don't think he'd ever seen someone that big before—and the man stepped off the sidewalk onto the street to let us pass. I thought that was a bit odd, until I realized that's the way it was in Mississippi. Anytime a black person passed a white person on the street, he or she made sure to give the white person the right of way.

Jean was in line at the grocery store once, getting ready to buy a whole bunch of food, when a black man in front of her said, "Here, ma'am, you go ahead of me."

She looked and saw he had just a couple of items. "No, that wouldn't be fair," she said. But he wouldn't take no for an answer. He got out of her way and wouldn't get back in the checkout line until she went through. I think he was afraid of getting into trouble with the locals if he didn't.

It was all a bit of a shock to me because I had come from such a different place. When I was growing up, nobody ever talked about race or religion. No black families lived in Haddam, so maybe that's why race wasn't a topic of conversation. But it certainly was a topic down south. Mississippi was probably the worst of it, but we saw segregation in Arkansas too. It wasn't just in train cars. There were separate bathrooms, separate restaurants—a real separation in how people lived their daily lives.

When David and Susan were young, they went to grade school for a time in West Helena, Arkansas. They still remember the separate drinking fountains the kids had to use while they were at school. No one at the school ever explained why, so our kids just couldn't understand what the different fountains were there for.

Susan was born in 1955, so the civil rights movement in this country was just getting started. Martin Luther King Jr.'s famous speech at the March on Washington wouldn't happen until 1963, but things were already stirring when we were living in the South. By the time sit-ins and protests started to be covered regularly in the news during the 1960s, we were living up north, near Kansas City. Still, as we watched coverage of the march across the bridge in Selma, Alabama, and the passage of the Voting Rights Act of 1965, we couldn't help but think about some of the things we'd seen during the short time we lived in the region. It gave us a different perspective from some in our area on what was happening.

Not too long after Susan was born, we started thinking more about how we wanted to raise our children. When we had only David and he was still young, we didn't mind all the moving from place to place. But then we had two kids, and then David started school, followed by Susan a few years later. Jean never complained about the unconventional life we were leading, but she started to become concerned about pulling the kids out of school every month or two.

Every time we picked up and moved on, Jean had to enroll the kids in a new school in a new town. She had to make sure to take their records with us and keep up with their progress and what they had learned already. A school in, say, New Hampshire might not be teaching the same things as one in North Carolina. We started to wonder: Was our traveling life what we really wanted for our family?

A Short History of Dodge City, Kansas
37° 45' 35" N, 100° 01' 06" W

THE TOWN NOW CALLED DODGE CITY was once a stop along the Santa Fe Trail, which served as a busy commercial route across unorganized territory in the nineteenth century, from Independence, Missouri, in the east to Santa Fe, New Mexico, in the west. The area was first known to settlers as Fort Mann, which was decimated by an Indian attack in 1848. It then went through a few more names before it became Fort Dodge in 1865, built by the military to provide protection along the trail during the Indian Wars.

Named after the nearby fort, Dodge City is famous for once being a wild frontier town of the Old West. In the late 1800s, after the railroad was built through town, it was well-known as the top place to go for driving cattle and hunting buffalo. Naturally, that attracted cowboys of all stripes. Dodge City got a reputation as a place where law and order was difficult to maintain, despite the fact that Marshal Wyatt Earp and others did their best to break up gunfights and chase away bad guys. The Boot Hill Cemetery just outside of town was known as a place where the marshals put those who refused to toe the line.

Today, the Boot Hill Museum, named after that infamous cemetery and located on Wyatt Earp Boulevard (the main road through town), is a testament to the location's Wild West past, complete with staged gunfights and "medicine shows" (where snake oil salesmen peddle their magic cure-alls) that take place along a recreation of old Front Street. Though the real saloons and gunslingers are long gone, farming and cattle-ranching are still a big part of what drives Dodge City today.

Family Values

Jean and I have certain values that we tried to teach our kids. We taught them to respect their elders. When they met someone new or somebody came over to visit, we wanted them to act as though they were glad to see the person (whether they were or not). Be friendly and treat people right—those were the main things we wanted our kids to learn. Next in importance was to do their best in school and get a good education to prepare them for their future. They took to those lessons overall. There were arguments here and there, and one of them might get sent to their room once in a while, but they weren't troublemakers. We were lucky in that we had really good kids.

It helped that we didn't have to raise them alone. To me and Jean, being part of the survey party had always felt like living with our extended family. Once we had children of our own, it felt even more like that. You never had to keep close track of your kids, because you knew they were always around someplace with other adults looking out for them. If Jean or I happened to see someone else's kids fighting or fussing, we would break it up or send them home. Others would do the same for ours. Everybody helped raise everybody else's kids.

The kids in the survey party had their squabbles from time to time, but they were all friends and played together. It was a good thing, too, because making friends at school could be hard for David and Susan. They were having to change schools several times a year.

As Susan got older, she had a group of girlfriends on the survey who played together. It was easy for David to make friends among the kids in the party, too, but he also used to hang out with some of the workers from time to time.

One guy, an observer named Bob Price, really took a liking to David. We were working in Fairfax, Virginia, at the time. Bob nicknamed David "J. Fred Muggs," after the chimpanzee that was a mascot on the *Today Show* in the mid- to late 1950s. He had some free time one Saturday and asked if he could take David to visit the zoo in Washington, DC, a good half hour's drive away. We let them go, but Jean worried the whole time about them getting lost or into a car wreck or something. She wasn't so sure Bob was reliable. But he and David did just fine. The two of them just got along for some reason.

About fifteen families with kids traveled together in the survey party. You'd expect it to be tough, but we didn't experience a lot of friction, even though we had so many families living in close quarters.

For a time, Jean and I lived next door to Frank and Frances Fencel, our best friends. Frank was the one who had stood up for me at our wedding. One day it was hot, and we both had the windows open on our trailers, no more than ten feet apart. I heard Frank asking Frances where something was. Frances told him she didn't know. Well, earlier that day I'd heard him say where he was going to put it, so I yelled over to them, "I'm sorry to have to tell you this, Frank, but you left it in the cupboard!" And I was right. That just shows you how close we lived.

We always lock our doors now, but back then nobody ever locked their trailers or worried about leaving things outside. That's the way it was in most of these small towns where we lived—not just for those of us in the survey party, but for everyone. People always felt safe.

The only time I can remember us having any trouble was in Kimball, Nebraska, when a drunken man came up to the door of our trailer and wanted to come inside. Even he didn't really cause much trouble, just a bit of a disturbance. We told him to get lost, and he did.

As our family got bigger, so did our trailer. We had a small trailer by the time David was born. When we had Susan, we got a bigger one. That's how it went as long as I was with the survey: the kids kept growing, and we kept trading up to larger trailers with more bells and whistles. It was just easier on the family that way.

Living that close together isn't for everyone, but we made it work. A bedroom in the back of the trailer had two bunks where the kids slept. You could pull shut a partition when you wanted separation, like when we'd put the kids to bed at night but still be up ourselves. We had a hide-a-bed in front—we pulled it out of the couch to make an extra bed—and that's where Jean and I slept. If the whole family was inside at once, we'd be right on top of each other, but at the time, no one seemed to mind. Everybody we knew, everybody around us, lived basically the same way, so the kids didn't know any different.

Besides, I never thought it made any difference where a person lived. You can be happy living in a small space just as much as in a big space, if you have the right mindset.

Being on top of each other had its upside, too. The field party was in Freeport, Texas, the first time we got a television set—the old kind, where you had to put up your own antenna. There was a pole set up near the trailers, and we had to put the antenna up there ourselves. It needed some height—twenty or twenty-five feet in the air—to get a signal. Whenever we left a location, we had to climb up and take the antenna down. It came apart and would travel with us from place to place.

It was a twenty-one-inch Zenith television that we bought, blond in color, with a little speaker on top that would fold out. It's funny to think about, in light of the huge flat screens of today with their high-resolution, but we thought we really had something at the time. We'd take the TV out of its case and put it on a little stand to watch it.

This was in the mid- to late 1950s, when they were really starting to make some entertaining shows. David still remembers the family sitting together on the couch to watch *The Ed Sullivan Show*. The reception was often pretty bad—a lot of snow—and you'd have to get up from time to time to adjust the antenna in one direction or another to get a signal. It was kind of a pain, but it was worth it. We had some good times together, gathering around that old TV.

The kitchen inside the trailer was pretty decent, too, even though it was small. I always ate with the family before I left for work, and then I'd take lunch with me. Jean did all the cooking then. Now she and I have switched, and I do most of the cooking at home; but back then, I could barely boil an egg. I did some cooking in Alaska, but it was nothing fancy—mostly just opening up some canned food and putting it on a plate. I didn't start really learning to cook more than pancakes until later in life.

With young David and newborn Susan in 1955

⋇

I didn't worry about much of anything back then. I'm not a worrying person by nature, but I also don't think there was much to be concerned about. My job was pretty secure. The government had a civil service pension I knew I'd be able to retire on. I didn't worry when the kids went out to play. They could run around wherever they wanted or play in the street, because there was no traffic. You didn't worry about crime. Things were just different in those days.

The only thing there was to be really concerned about was the kids' education. David enrolled in school for the first time in Gorham, New Hampshire, which had a good school system. But three months later, we moved to Ahoskie, North Carolina, for a month or so. David was enrolled in school there, and we found out that he was way ahead of his class. It took some time for them to catch up. But he wasn't too upset, because he fell in love with his first-grade teacher in Ahoskie.

Moving every month or two or three made it difficult to know whether the kids were getting a good education, which was important to both of us. We wanted them to be able to go to college one day. Because of that, we gave them a lot of help at home—especially Jean. We always took an interest in what David and Susan were learning and what sort of school activities they were taking part in. They always came home and did their homework at the kitchen table. David was good at that. He would always do his homework and then go out and play. Susan often wanted to put things off to the last second, and yet she still did well in school. They were just different that way.

It wasn't just the educational part of school that could be hard for them. There was the social part too. Even though they had their friends from the survey party, they still had to find their place with a new group of kids at school each time we moved. Sometimes it was tough—more on Susan than on David, I think, but he had his troubles too.

One time in Tucumcari, New Mexico, David came running home from school after a kid tried to beat him up. He didn't want to have anything to do with that kid, but I told him he needed to go back out there and face him. "You're going to have to learn to stick up for yourself," I said. "You can't let people run over you." So he went back out and got into a little scrap with the kid, and he did okay.

On the other hand, there were some places that the kids really liked. David and Susan both went to school in Dodge City, Kansas—twice. Dodge City was one of the bigger cities we lived in, and they loved both the school and their teachers, as well as the town itself.

Moving around so much offered one great advantage: the kids got to see all these different places and have all these experiences that most kids didn't get. If there was something special to visit or do, we would take them when we had time. In Dodge City, for example, a simulation of an old Western town was set up, where they reenacted gunfights and things like that. The kids loved walking into the saloon and slamming those old-fashioned swinging doors, like they were a big deal in town. They thought that was really something.

When we moved from place to place, Jean would take the kids in our car and go on ahead. She'd do that because it wasn't really safe for the kids to ride in the trailer when it was being pulled. Plus, I always wanted her to go first so I didn't have to look back to see if she was coming.

I would use a government vehicle to tow the trailer, which took a bit longer because I couldn't go as fast. But that was okay, because when I'd drive into a new town, Jean and the kids would already be there, in the park or someplace, usually eating ice cream. I'd wave at them as I went by.

The kids always wanted ice cream, because we were so often in warm places. When we bought one of our cars back then, I told Jean that we ought to get air-conditioning. "Naw, we don't need air-conditioning," she said, so we bought it without. That was one of the biggest mistakes I've ever made in my life. We were in some really hot places, and we spent a lot of time sweating in that car.

In fact, about the only time we encountered real winter weather was when we went back home for a visit. That was another reason why we needed a car—so we could go back to Missouri and Kansas for vacations and holidays. One time, when we were driving from Dodge City to visit Jean's sister in St. Joseph, Missouri, we hit a big blizzard. We were only about thirty miles from where we needed to be, so we figured we could still make it. We just wanted to get there, you know?

Well, it got so bad, so fast, that we couldn't see where we were going. Ice had formed on the windshield so thick, I couldn't even brush it off with the windshield wiper. We saw the lights of some motel up ahead, and I told Jean, "Boy, we should stop and get a room." But we didn't do it. We were so close . . .

Jean's sister lived in a farming area, in a house with a long driveway. We made it to the entrance of that driveway, but that was as far as we could go. There was just too much snow on the driveway to drive up to the house. So we got out of the car, left it where it was, and walked the rest of the way up.

Driving through that snowstorm was the stupidest thing I'd ever done in my life, because I knew better. It would've been one thing if it were just Jean and I, but we had Susan and David in the backseat. We were starting to realize: now that we had kids, we couldn't just do everything the way we had been doing it.

A young David and Susan pose with the traveling homes of the survey team

When we were getting ready to leave Dodge City, Jean picked David up at school so she could talk to his teachers. One of them, who was also David's basketball coach, said to her, "I wish David were staying here. I'd like to follow his career in basketball." He was a pretty good athlete back then, not just at basketball but a solid baseball player, too.

When David got into sports, I got into coaching. I helped coach David's baseball team in Jacksonville, Arkansas. In the same trailer park where we were staying, there was a sergeant from the nearby military base. He and I put the team together, because we both had sons who wanted to play and there was no team already in place. The hardest part was rounding up the kids. We had a couple of kids from the survey party, but that wasn't enough for a team. We had to get some locals involved, too. A lot of the parents around there weren't very good at taking their kids to activities, so we had to get after them to make sure they showed up. Sometimes we even had to pick them up at their homes and bring them to the games and practices ourselves. It was worth it, though, because David really liked playing.

The whole survey party took an interest in the kids' games, and David ended up with quite a following. I think that started when we were in Jacksonville. Practically everybody in the survey party would come out and watch him play on Saturdays. We made quite a crowd with just our people.

I also helped coach his Little League team one summer when we were in Kimball, Nebraska. David was the youngest player. That was where he first learned to pitch. One day, when the team ran out of pitchers, the head coach called in David, who usually played third base. Jean got very nervous. She was afraid David wouldn't do very well and would get upset about it. He was always a pretty competitive kid. But he struck out three in a row, and the team went on to win the game.

That was a big day. After we won, one of David's friends from the survey party picked him up and carried him around on his shoulders. David was only twelve years old, and it was one of the highlights of his young life. He went on to pitch more games after that.

We won the league that year, which was great, but mostly I just liked working with the kids, whether they were good athletes or not. We had this one little guy on the team who was not very coordinated. I was afraid to put him in the outfield because I figured somebody might hit a ball out there that would knock him in the head. That's how bad he was. He couldn't throw very well, and he didn't always remember to pay attention. But he could catch the ball if he saw it coming, so I decided to make him a catcher.

The team had two notable pitchers, David and another left-handed kid, and both were really good for their age. They threw the ball hard at this kid, and it always ended up in his mitt. But then he'd have to walk the ball halfway back to the mound before he could throw it back to them. He'd never played ball before, and I'm not sure he even had any interest; I think his parents wanted him to play. But he did pretty well as a catcher. We made it work, and he was a good addition to our team.

I found I really liked coaching. If I had gone to college, that's probably what I would have done. For a while, I really thought about getting my degree. When I came out of Alaska, I had extra money. Jean and I talked it over, and we decided I would stay where I was.

I wonder sometimes if that was a mistake or not. I probably made as much money working for the government as I would have made teaching, but money isn't all that matters. Choosing the right job is about doing what you enjoy doing, and I really liked what I was doing. I liked being outdoors and traveling. And, well, I never really liked school. I didn't like being indoors or having to learn about a lot of stuff I wasn't interested in. I think I would have enjoyed being a coach, but getting through more school would have been hard.

We spent a lot of time around military bases in the late 1950s because that was when the party started to survey a different kind of site. The Cold War was well underway, and the U.S. government had built missile silos in different parts of the country to defend against a Russian attack. We traveled around to a lot of those places and surveyed the missile sites for the military.

I ended up on the East Coast only a few times throughout my career with the Coast Survey, and this was one of them. We had been working in Kittanning, Pennsylvania, when the boss sent a small group of us to Buffalo, New York, to put geodetic controls on missile sites. I was separated from my family the whole time the party was there, for about a month and a half.

Jean and the kids stayed behind in Kittanning, because our boss didn't typically set up a full camp or send out the families when just a subparty was assigned to do a smaller job.

There were a lot of missiles in Buffalo—small Nike missiles, located on top of buildings and in government facilities around the city. One building had a huge radar system, which had to be turned off before we were allowed to work from the tower that was close by. We never did learn exactly what the radar was used for, but we were told that it was so strong, it could have fried us.

Missile sites were priority projects at the time, so the Coast Survey did a number of them. I was always amazed by how much the government spent to protect the country. Those silos obviously weren't cheap to build. Buffalo was unusual in that the missiles were housed in a decent-sized city. A lot of the larger missiles and silos were in pretty remote places, such as Nebraska, Kansas, and Wyoming. The government would build big fences around an area in the middle of a field on land that they often bought from a local farmer. Everybody in town knew the secret, but if you weren't from around there, you'd never think to look in these places.

The underground facilities used to house the missiles were well-built. Years later, the government took all those missiles out but left the silos behind. Farmers began using them to store grain just because they were there. There wasn't much else to do with them.

Missouri was an important location for missile sites. We surveyed about eight locations in the state, mostly around Whiteman Air Force Base, about seventy miles from Kansas City. We set up camp in Knob Noster, right nearby. There wasn't much around there, but we were able to enroll David and Susan at a school where the base kids went.

Around that time, David got it in his head that he wanted a saxophone. He thought it would be fun to learn how to play for some reason. I wasn't so sure I wanted to listen to him learn saxophone in our trailer, so I figured I better make sure he was serious about getting good at it before I let him have one. I told him he could have a saxophone if he saved up his money and paid for it himself. When he heard that, he decided he didn't really want a saxophone after all. Later on, I felt bad about not getting him that saxophone. He could have been the next Tommy Dorsey! Now we'll never know.

While I was stationed in Knob Noster in 1962, Karen was born. Because of what had happened with Susan's birth, the doctor insisted that Jean have another caesarean section. This time, I was there to drive her to the hospital, in Sedalia, Missouri, the next town over to the east.

Jean's mother had come to stay with us in our trailer to help Jean out and take care of the two older kids while we were away. While Jean was in the hospital, her mother insisted on a few changes. "You're old enough to get dressed yourself, Sue," she announced one morning. It was an awful shock for Susan, because Jean had always dressed her. I think Susan was pretty happy to have her mom back home after that.

Around the time Jean came home from the hospital, public warnings went out across the country: be ready for a potential attack by the Russians. The Bay of Pigs invasion, the failed attempt to overthrow Fidel Castro in Cuba, had happened just the previous year. Both of our older kids were in school, and we were advised that leaving them there during an emergency would keep them safest. The students all had to practice their drills by getting under the desks when the warnings came.

We didn't know what to expect, but there wasn't really anything we could do besides wait. So we waited, and watched the television for updates. Obviously, things turned out okay in the end, but it was pretty scary for a while. It was just a couple of years later, while we were living in Dodge City for the second time, that President Kennedy was shot and killed. That hit everyone in the country pretty hard, whether they supported his politics or not.

In 1962, the same year that Karen was born, I was promoted to a new position in the survey party: computer. I was now in charge of computing the data sent in from our field observers' daily observations. I also had the responsibility of scheduling the night crew—anywhere from fifteen to thirty people. I would take all their data, compute it, and make sure it met our specifications. At the end of the job, I'd send the data to Washington. Because there was no such thing as fax or email then, we had to send all our data by mail.

By this time, the U.S. Coast and Geodetic Survey was under the Department of Commerce. The survey office had wanted me to establish a geodetic position on the Space Needle, which had been built especially for the World's Fair in Seattle that year, but I turned the job down. I didn't want to deal with all that rainfall. I'd been through Seattle more than once on my way to Alaska, and the weather was bad every time. The guy who was doing the computing for our party said he was interested in the role. So I took his job, and he went off to Seattle to do mine.

When I switched to computing, I started working out of a trailer with the boss. It was more like office work, and I liked it okay for a while even though I really preferred going out into the field. I've always liked being outside. But computing was a better job with better pay. And even if it wasn't quite as fun as scaling mountainsides, it sure was a lot easier.

From the very beginning of my years on the survey crew, everything seemed to progress in my favor. I was hired right out of high school to be on the crew that built the towers. Then I was on a crew that worked nights to do the observations from the towers—first as a recorder, then as an observer. Then I was able to make more money as a computer, during the day and out of a trailer, when that was best for my growing family. I was very fortunate that everything just fell into place for me for some reason. Someone was looking out for me, I think.

Being a computer positioned me for the next career move I would make, which was especially good for my family. A new field office was being set up in Kansas City, and the man in charge was Captain Robert Earl—the man who had been captain of the NOAA's *Pathfinder* when I was on Nunivak Island. Captain Earl had been the one to offer me a whiskey back then, after I had so much trouble getting aboard his ship, but he was about to give me something even better—something life-changing.

I had heard about a job opening up in the new field office, which would oversee all the survey work in the Midwest. I was working in Minnesota at the time, and the captain and his wife were in the area so he could inspect the survey party. This happened every year: somebody from headquarters would come out to check the money in the safe we traveled with and make sure everything was in accordance with government regulations. This time, Jean and I invited Captain Earl and his wife in for dinner at our trailer.

I wanted to tell Captain Earl the reason I wanted the job: to get my family settled somewhere. Otherwise, I was going to have to buy a house someplace and then travel back and forth to it in between jobs. That would mean being separated from my family while I was out in the field, for months at a time sometimes. I didn't want to do that, so I was looking for other opportunities.

Jean and I had been talking about it for a while by then, and we knew it was time. David was in the fifth grade, and Susan was in second. Karen was young yet, but it was just going to get harder and harder for the kids to change schools so often. Now that we had three children, stability seemed even more important than ever.

Captain Earl seemed to like me, and he understood my position. Still, we had to wait months before we would know if I got the job. The captain had originally hoped that a guy working for him, Gerald "Pink" Randall (who was also a good friend of ours) would get the job. Pink was a grade too high for the position, however, so headquarters wouldn't let him take it. Meanwhile, I was the right grade, so finally the word came through: I got the job.

I was going to be transferred to the Kansas City field office, where I would work on the Mark Maintenance program. That meant Jean, the kids, and I could finally settle down in one place. We could sell our trailer and buy an actual house. It would be the first time since Jean and I had been married that we could live that way. It was going to be a whole new way of life.

David, Susan, and Karen with their Easter baskets:
Jean and I always did our best to keep up childhood traditions, even on the road.

A Short History of Kansas City, Missouri
39° 05' 59" N, 94° 34' 42" W

LOCATED ALONG THE KANSAS—MISSOURI BORDER, Kansas City played a prime role during America's westward expansion. Set where the Kansas and Missouri rivers meet, and along the route of the historic Santa Fe, California, and Oregon trails, it became both a steamboat landing and a supply point for traders and travelers during the mid-1800s.

The unique location of Kansas City also played an important role in the Civil War that broke out in the 1860s. Missouri had been a slave state since its statehood in 1821. Kansas, on the other hand—which didn't enter the Union until 1861, just before the war—included many Free-Staters who opposed slavery. In fact, Kansas City served as a headquarters for the Union Army. During the war, conflicts erupted in the region. The Confederates won two major battles in the suburbs just outside of the city, in the town of Independence (which would later become known as the hometown of President Harry S. Truman), even as Kansas City remained under Union control.

The city grew rapidly, in both population and territory, after the end of the war. Today, it is the largest city in the state of Missouri and the nation's twenty-third largest city by total area.

Kansas City, Here We Come

WEST HELENA, ARKANSAS, WAS THE LAST place we lived as part of the survey party. I still have a record of the work we did there—a newspaper article in the local *Memphis Press-Scimitar*, titled "Coast & Geodetic Survey Brings Joy to Surveyors and Engineers." The paper shows a picture of me alongside my boss, Lieutenant Robert Trauschke. The reporter, Mrs. Chris Griffin, wrote: "The 27-man party is one of many that methodically roam the nation in a nomadic way of life from the Great Lakes to the Gulf; from the Atlantic to the Pacific and in Alaska and Hawaii." Of course, my "nomadic way of life" was about to end.

Jean and I took our trailer and our family and moved to Kansas City, Missouri, in December 1964. Going from Arkansas to Missouri at that time of year was something of a shock. Remember, our survey party did most of our work in warm places—up north in the summers, down south in the winters—so we hadn't dealt with much cold weather up to that point. Kansas City, when we arrived in December, was cold as heck. Thankfully, I had just bought a new trailer with a big gas furnace, so we were warm as long as we stayed inside.

After so many years of trailer living, we were going to be in one place for a while. We knew we wanted to find a house, but we needed time to look for the right one. So we moved into a trailer park in east Kansas City in time for Christmas. Then, after the holiday break, I started my new job and David and Susan started at the local school.

Karen was only about three years old at the time, so she spent her days at the trailer park with Jean. She was the only one who didn't seem to mind the cold. She could run around in the wintertime with her coat unbuttoned and no hat or gloves on. All the other little kids in the trailer park were catching colds, but Karen hardly ever got sick.

The trailer park in Kansas City was a big place, and there were lots of folks around. One of our neighbors had a German shepherd in a fenced area next to their trailer. The German shepherd had recently had puppies, and one day Karen got it into her head that she wanted one. So she opened the gate, walked right in there with that big dog, took one of her puppies, and walked out again. The dog's owner saw Karen and brought her home.

When Jean and I found out what happened, it scared the heck out of us. Karen was just this little, tow-headed thing—she used to have white-blond hair that Jean would cut real short—and we couldn't help but imagine what that dog could have done to her. But Karen wasn't afraid at all. She had played with her friends in that yard, and she knew that dog, so she wasn't worried about it. And that German shepherd didn't bother her at all. She was a little upset, however, that she didn't get to keep the puppy.

Even though Karen had her friends, the trailer park never felt like a very friendly place to live. It certainly wasn't like the survey community that we had known so well. We also realized pretty quickly that the local school system wasn't very good, so we wanted to get out of there as soon as possible. We stayed in the trailer park until the spring, when we found our very first house.

Back in those days, most people didn't have checking accounts. If you saved any money, you usually kept it in cash or bought government bonds that you'd hide somewhere in your home. That's what I did. Whenever we had a little extra cash over the years, I'd buy a bond. I had a little tin box where I'd put the bonds for safekeeping, and we'd take that with us in the trailer from place to place. Over the years, I had stored up quite a few of those bonds, so when it came time to buy our first house, I cashed them in and used the money for our down payment. The total cost of the house was about twenty-two thousand dollars, and I still remember counting out that down payment. It was all of about six thousand dollars.

We bought a three-bedroom, split-level house with a basement and a two-car garage. David got his own room, and the girls shared. It was on a corner lot, so it had a big front yard and a small backyard with a patio. Compared with the way we'd been living, it offered a huge amount of space. Even so, Jean originally liked another house that was even bigger. The problem was, it was two thousand dollars more.

At the time, we were making about ten thousand dollars a year. I told Jean that if she really wanted that house, she was gonna have to give up something else. We wouldn't be able to go out as much or do as many things, because all our extra money would go to paying for that house. She thought about that and finally decided no, she could live with the smaller house, especially since it didn't feel "small" to us at all.

The house was practically new. It had been owned by only one couple before us, and they had lived there less than two years. They left it as neat as a pin. We assumed their loan, which had a pretty low rate, so our payments were only about one hundred dollars a month. After we bought the house, we had some money left over to have a little fun with.

Because we'd been living in trailers for years, Jean and I didn't have hardly anything to put in a house. Trailers come with everything built in—the beds, the kitchen table, even the couch—so we needed a whole houseful of new stuff. We traveled about fifty miles north to St. Joseph, Missouri, because somebody told us that you could get good buys up there. We went to a big furniture place and had the best time with this salesman there. Every time we agreed to buy something, he would throw in something else for free—we bought a couch, so he gave us a picture to go with it. I'd never had anyone give me a deal like that. I think he realized that we had a lot to buy, and he wanted to get *all* our business.

That furniture salesman really set us up well. We went in there with practically nothing, and by the time we left, we had everything we needed. The store sent a truck to our empty house, and by the time the truck pulled away, the house was filled. Getting to outfit a whole house all at once doesn't happen very often. We had a lot of fun that day, picking out all the new things we wanted to live with.

The only thing that was already in the house was a large mural painted on the wall in the dining area. It had this design going through it, with colored flags and white columns, and it really made the room. There was a nice fireplace in the family room too, along with hardwood floors secured with pegs instead of nails—it was just a beautiful floor. We added a dark green couch and two red easy chairs, the most comfortable chairs I have ever had. I haven't had a good chair to sit in since we got rid of those.

I always loved that room, but in the trailer, Jean and I had been sleeping on a hide-a-bed, so we were especially happy about being able to buy an actual bed. It would be the first time in many years that we got to sleep regularly on one of those. It really was going to be a different way of life.

Setting foot in that house for the first time, the kids were beyond excited. After living their entire lives in trailers, they thought they were moving into a mansion. That's what they kept saying as they explored the new house: "We're living in a mansion! We're living in a mansion!" It wasn't a "mansion," of course, but it was a really nice house, much larger than the trailer.

We had upgraded to a larger trailer only a year or so before, but even that was nothing like having an entire house to live in. With three kids by then, I'd chosen the biggest trailer I could get: a forty-six-footer with that gas furnace and central air-conditioning—the whole works. The total length once you hooked it up to a van or truck to pull it was about sixty-five feet. Driving anything over that length required permits. Different states required different permits, and I didn't want to get involved in that mess— especially since we traveled all over the place. That meant I couldn't go any bigger than forty-six feet.

When we bought the house, we didn't need the trailer anymore, so I put it up for sale. Unfortunately, I had it up for sale for a while, and wasn't getting much action. The only person who showed any interest was Gilbert "Gibby" Berdine, a friend on the field party. Gilbert told Jean that he wanted the trailer but wouldn't have the money for about two months. I had to think about that offer for a while.

Gibby was a real character. When I first met him, in Somerset, Kentucky, he was a perfect gentleman. But I had heard a story about him working in Las Vegas, where he had gambled away his trailer and his car in a single day. He won them both back two weeks later, but that story still gave me pause.

The bank advised us not to sell to him, but I finally decided to go with my gut. Even though Gibby liked to gamble, if he said he would pay us, I believed that he would. "Let him have the trailer if he wants it," I said. No one else was offering me anything for it anyway. And he did pay us a couple of months later, just like he said he would. Later in life, Gibby and I became good friends when we worked together in the Coast Survey's main office, in Rockville, Maryland.

I still lost money on the deal, because the trailer was so new. If I had known I was going to get the job and buy a house in Kansas City, I wouldn't have bothered to buy the top of the line. But I didn't worry about it too much, especially since the house was such a big hit with the kids. At the same time, I think the kids kind of missed the survey party. It was just us living there, which was the way we wanted it. Still, they missed being with their friends all the time. It was something they had to get used to. Other than that, there weren't any regrets.

We had chosen the town of Independence, Missouri, a suburb just outside of Kansas City, because it was part of the Raytown School District—the best school system around. In fact, we were right on the dividing line. Our kids went to the Raytown schools, but our neighbor's kids across the street went to the Independence schools. We figured all that out and picked the house carefully. Now that we were settling down, Jean and I were determined that the kids would get the best possible education.

Independence is Harry Truman country. The library of our thirty-third president is there—one of my favorite of all the presidential libraries I've visited. New exhibits are going on there all the time. One of the unique spots in town is Clinton's Soda Fountain, whose claim to fame is giving Harry his first job as a boy. Independence is where Truman grew up, where he and his wife returned after he left the White House, and where he died just a few years after we moved to town.

When we were traveling all the time, Jean was never able to work because we were never in the same place long enough for her to get a job. But when we settled in Independence, once all the kids were in school, she got a part-time job at a movie theater, organizing parties, ordering supplies, and doing the bookkeeping. Jean's boss at the movie theater lived close to the house where Truman lived with his wife, Bess—a surprisingly modest, older home on the corner of a typical suburban street.

When Truman passed away in 1972, we had a ringside seat for the events that followed. We were able to stand on the street outside Jean's boss's house and watch as all the dignitaries came by to pay their respects, including former President Lyndon Johnson and his wife and daughters. We heard that President Nixon came by too, but unfortunately we missed him. Everybody in town was saying that if Truman had known that Nixon had been invited into his house, he would have rolled over in his grave.

I had been to Kansas City before we moved there. It was a larger city than we were used to, but I had always liked it. Even though my new job had me working out of the Kansas City office, I wasn't in the office all that often. I was no longer traveling with a survey party, but travel was still a big part of my job.

The office in Kansas City was in charge of organizing all the field parties that were working throughout the Midwest. Captain Earl, who had been in charge of setting up the new office, left shortly after he hired me. But to me, it didn't matter much who was in charge. My work on the Mark Maintenance program involved traveling to different triangulation stations throughout the region in order to preserve geodetic positions for marks in my assigned area.

Whenever a survey party had finished their work and were leaving a location, they left a mark behind—a bronze circle encased in concrete that read: *Triangulation Station, U.S. Coast and Geodetic Survey. For information write to the Director, Washington 25, D.C. $250 fine or imprisonment for disturbing the mark.*

Sometimes, however, those marks couldn't stay where the survey party had left them. Maybe a road was being moved or a new one built, so the highway department would call us up and say we needed to move the mark out of the way. Or maybe a farmer would decide he didn't want the mark in his yard any longer because he wanted to plant something there. When things like that happened, I was sent out to fix the problem.

When I traveled to these sites, I had to bring all my equipment with me. I still used a theodolite, although it was a smaller version of what I'd started out using years before—a Wild T2 instead of a Wild T3, both of which were made in Sweden. I would start by finding a new place where the mark could go. After I did the calculations to record the new position, I'd have to physically move the mark. That meant digging up the concrete marker, pulling it out of the ground, and then setting it in the new spot.

It was different from my work with the survey party, because I was traveling more often—and by myself. Often, I would enlist somebody to help me: some local guy who was willing to work for a few days, or someone from the highway department if he was available. Instead of staying in one place for a month or two, I'd travel to a different place weekly. I covered sites all throughout the Midwest, as far east as Indiana and Ohio, as far west as Colorado, and as far north as Minnesota. Later on, the territory was split up, with someone else covering the Chicago region and then a third guy in Minnesota. But in the beginning, I covered all that area on my own.

I was on the road a lot of the time. I would try to make it home on weekends, but sometimes I had to travel so far that I'd have to be away for two weeks at a time. So I was traveling more than ever, running all over the place. The difference was, my family got to stay in one place, which was good for us in the long run.

Living near a large city gave our family the opportunity to do some different kinds of things. When the movie *The Sound of Music* came out, we took David and Susan to go see it. Karen was too young, so we left her home with a babysitter, but the rest of us got dressed up and went to a theater in downtown Kansas City. Like a lot of those old movie houses, this one was pretty grand—an attractive place with a large staircase in the middle of the lobby. I never will forget Susan, in her pretty dress, looking around that big, grand lobby and saying, "Oh my, I feel like a princess."

Of course, not everything was so easy to adjust to. David was in sixth grade when we moved, which meant he was able to start junior high the following year, and this time he would be able to stay at the same school for a while. But the school was much bigger than the small, countryside schools he'd attended. He had always been a pretty good athlete, but now he was up against bigger kids and more competition. He just wasn't as quick as some of them, so he had to get used to not being the star anymore.

No place is perfect, but the kids adjusted pretty well and pretty quickly, as kids often do. Karen would have to move just once more as a student, but both David and Sue finished out high school in the same school district, just as we had wanted. When we were traveling with the survey party, none of the kids ever complained about moving so often. Yet they really seemed to take to their new environment, which told me it was the right place for them.

⁂

Our family stayed in Kansas City for almost ten years, and we would have stayed longer. After working in Mark Maintenance for a number of years, I moved to a new job in operations, where I organized and provided support to the parties in the field. Fortunately, that meant leaving the field and working out of an office most of the day. It was for the same pay, but with an easier schedule that meant I didn't have to be away from my family all week long. At that point in my life, it was all about getting off the road. After years of traveling together, and then years of me traveling alone, it was time for us all to be home together as much as possible.

Unfortunately, I didn't have that operations job for very long. Less than a year later, the Kansas City office closed and all Midwest operations were transferred to the main headquarters in Rockville, Maryland. That meant I had a choice: I could transfer to Maryland, or I could find a new job.

I didn't want to leave Kansas City. I felt like a Midwest guy and didn't think being on the East Coast would suit me. Plus, I'd made a lot of good friends there: Paul Brown, who was chief of operations. Leon Smith, who was in charge of the Mark Maintenance program and my direct boss. Gerald Randall, or "Pink" as we called him, I think because he had a pinkish complexion. Andy Webb, from Warrensburg, Missouri, who was always trying to find out your business and liked to talk about how lucky I was.

"A lot of these guys that come off the survey parties don't have nothing at all," Andy pointed out. That was true. A lot of people on the survey spent everything they made, because what they made wasn't a lot. But Jean and I had been careful about saving money, enough so we could buy the house we lived in. It was nice of him to notice, I guess, but I really didn't think he needed to talk about it. Still, we got along pretty well all the same.

Most of those men retired when the Kansas City office closed, but I was too young—the youngest one in the office. I had one kid in college, another about to start, and a third who still had high school to finish. At first, I tried to get my old job back so I could stay in Kansas City. On the Mark Maintenance program, because there was so much travel involved, I could be based out of anywhere within the territory. But someone else had already taken my old position.

Next I applied for a job with the Environmental Protection Agency in Kansas City. They were on the verge of hiring me when the government declared a hiring freeze. No one knew how long that was going to last, and I couldn't wait around to find out. So I took the transfer to Maryland.

From then on out, it was just office work. I would work for the Coast and Geodetic Survey for another ten years in Rockville, until I retired in 1985 at the age of fifty-five. During that time, I held just one position: running the Mark Maintenance program, the same one I had worked on in Kansas City. At one point, I had sixteen people working under me. I was also in charge of the Geodetic Advisor program, which sent people out to different places to train groups in surveying work.

I never worked in the field again, not for any extended period of time anyway. Working from an office was very different. There were some memorable moments, like the morning I was waiting for the elevator while standing next to a Greek woman and a Turkish man. When the elevator arrived, I stepped on and the Greek lady followed. We held the door, but the Turk wouldn't get into the elevator. Their countries had no love for each other, so they didn't either. I learned something new and interesting that day, but in general, I found office work to be a hard adjustment.

I just really liked working in the field and getting the chance to make a home in a new place every month or so. I had never grown tired of traveling, and I kind of missed it. A love of travel is in the blood, I think. Most of my fellow surveyors liked what they were doing and how they lived. I never heard anybody complain about it. When someone stopped working on the field party, it was usually for a reason like mine: to take a job that would allow their family to settle down somewhere.

But that's how it is. As your life changes, your priorities change too. I missed traveling, but I got used to being in the office all day. At the end of the day, my family was the most important thing. It was just a better life for all of us.

Near retirement, in 1985, I worked with the International Boundary Commission to reestablish the boundary monument along the Minnesota–Canada border.

Afterword

WHEN I LEFT THE COAST AND Geodetic Survey in 1985, I had been working in Rockville, Maryland. In order to retire with full benefits, you had to be at least fifty-five years old and have thirty years of service. I had been working for the survey for so long, I already had my thirty years by the time I turned fifty-five. By then, I was tired of what I was doing, so I took the earliest opportunity to retire. I had gone as high in my line of work as I could go, and I'd been in the same position for twelve years. So it was time.

Things were changing anyway. When GPS came in, no one was interested in maintaining the database of geodetic positions any longer. In the beginning, they used our data to test the satellites and refine the GPS system, which was just for military use at first. Once the system was working well, though, you could just set it up and get a position instantly. My job got pretty quiet after that, around 1984, because it was no longer necessary to maintain the marks. People stopped calling, and the letters stopped coming. I retired about a year later.

I didn't stop working entirely. I took on a contract project with the U.S. Boundary Commission, which took me to northern Minnesota to supervise a crew that was reestablishing the boundary monuments along the U.S.–Canada border. It was wintertime when I got there, and the temperature fell to –35 degrees Fahrenheit. It was this sort of weather that had destroyed the monuments in the first place. The permafrost would get so bad, it raised the monuments right out of the ground.

The ground was pretty frozen when we were there, but I still found it scary when we had to drive our vehicles, which were loaded down with equipment, across a lake to get to several monuments that needed to be replaced. We made it across okay, but one of our trucks did get stuck in a peat bog later on and started sinking because it was so heavy. It was like that truck was in quicksand, and the crew had to unload everything quickly before it could get towed out.

Thankfully, I was just supervising, so I got to spend most of my time in the truck and out of the cold. That was my last real work adventure. By then, I think I was ready for it to be over.

⁓⍲⁓

When we traveled with the Coast Survey, I think my whole family learned how to be pretty resourceful. Having to pick up your life and move your home on a regular basis will have that effect. Still, I never could have imagined my kids would lead the lives they do now. I always hoped they would have good lives, but they've exceeded what I could have pictured for them. One of our biggest goals for our kids was to give them a good education, and all three of them ended up going to college, even though neither Jean nor I did.

Our kids had a pretty unusual upbringing, but all the moving around didn't seem to hurt any of the kids on the field party. All of them were smart, and every one went to college—every one that I know of, anyway. It's a credit to the people who worked the Coast Survey—all hard-working folks who cared about their kids and looked out for one another. That made all the difference, more than making up for the constant changes the kids went through.

After majoring in advertising and graduating from the University of Missouri with a degree in journalism, David started working at an advertising agency and then joined Pepsico. He kept climbing the corporate ladder and went on to become the cofounder, chairman, and CEO of

Yum! Brands, one of the world's largest restaurant companies. He and his wife, Wendy, have a daughter named Ashley and three grandkids, Audrey, Claire, and Luke.

Susan went to the University of Missouri for a time too, but then she went on to get a business degree, majoring in accounting, from the University of Maryland at College Park. She worked for an accounting firm based in Washington, DC, before becoming a regional controller at Life Care Centers of America, the largest privately held long-term care company in the country. She then moved to Ashburn, Virginia, to be closer to her sister and opened a clothing boutique named Sister's. After she closed that business, she moved to Scottsdale, Arizona, on a temporary job with her old company, Life Care Centers of America, and she worked with them as a division controller until her retirement.

Karen went to Frostburg State College and the University of Maryland at College Park before getting married. She worked for a computer company in Bethesda, Maryland, and she had two sons, Brian and Steven. Now she works as a patient coordinator for a well known plastic surgeon in Ashburn, whom she met in the ER after her son, Steven, was hit in the head with a golf club. She could tell when she visited the doctor's practice that he needed help, and she's been working with him for over seventeen years. Karen also has a grandchild, Brooks, which means Jean and I are great-grandparents to four children.

After our mothers passed away in the 1990s, Jean and I decided that, at our age, we better move closer to family. That was when we moved to Ashburn, Virginia, where Susan and Karen lived for a while. While we were there, Susan moved to Scottsdale, which is where we ended up too, after twelve years in Virginia.

When we were thinking about where we wanted to end up, we thought back over all the many places we had lived and what we'd liked and what we hadn't. We knew we didn't want to live in a big city, but a lot of the smaller towns where we'd been were gone by then. That's one thing that's really changed over the years: so many small towns, whittled away to almost nothing. That's why we never really considered going back home to Meadville or Haddam.

I didn't have much reason to return to Haddam once my parents passed away. I haven't been back for years now. Haddam today is like so many small towns across the country. The kids go off to college or to find jobs, just like I did, and they never come back for more than a visit. Many of these little farming towns have just deteriorated. The population shrinks and shrinks as the years go by, and those who remain are mostly older folks.

I bet you there's no more than one hundred people living in Haddam today. Main Street, which used to be so busy in my pool hall days, is nothing like it used to be. There's still a restaurant there, but it's not much of a business. People volunteer to cook dinners every once in a while for the locals, just so they have something to do.

Of all the places where I lived and worked while I was traveling with the Coast and Geodetic Survey, I bet no more than a handful are anything like what they used to be when we made our home there for a short while.

That's just the ways things go, I guess.

Acknowledgments

I WANT TO ACKNOWLEDGE MY WIFE, Jean, for putting up with me for sixty-nine years. She has been my partner through it all, inspiring me over the years and giving me three beautiful children, David, Susan, and Karen, whom I adore. Through her guidance, my life has improved, and she has played a large part in making our kids so successful.

I couldn't have asked for better daughters than Karen and Susan. They are both family-oriented people and the first ones to offer help whenever someone needs it. I admire them for the lives they lead and the people they have become.

One of my Christmas presents in 2017 from my son, David, and my daughter-in-law, Wendy, was a framed cover for a book they hoped I'd write someday about growing up and living in small towns throughout the country. They made arrangements for me to work with writer and editor Christa Bourg on the subject. She has been a true professional, and I enjoyed our time together very much.

Looking back over the years, I've had many ups and downs in my life. Remembering my life experiences for this book has made me realize how much I've accomplished and the many things I've experienced during nearly ninety years on this earth. Thanks to David and Wendy, I've gotten to do things that many people only dream of. These are some of the things I've done since retiring:

- Attend basketball games at Allen Field House at the University of Kansas at Lawrence.

- Attend the World Series at Progressive Field (formerly Jacobs Field) in Cleveland, Ohio.

- Attend the PGA Golf Tournament at Valhalla Country Club, including having lunch with my son, David, and Phil Mickelson.

- Take a fifteen-day bus trip through Europe.

- Go on a land and cruise tour of Alaska.

- Spend weekends in New York City, attending shows (favorite shows: The Will Rogers Follies and The Phantom of the Opera), and eating breakfast at Tavern on the Green in Central Park.

- Spend a weekend at Augusta National Golf Course in Georgia with my grandson, Brian.

- Attend a ceremony in Washington, DC, where David received the 2015 Horatio Alger award for his commitment to philanthropy.

- Attend the Kentucky Derby.

- Have dinner with David and Coach John Calipari of the University of Kentucky Wildcats.

- Attend basketball games at the KFC Yum! Center in Louisville, Kentucky, and even watch a practice with Louisville Cardinals Coach Rick Pitino.

- Attend basketball games at Rupp Arena, home of the Kentucky Wildcats, in Lexington, Kentucky, and receive a jersey signed by Coach Tabby Smith at a halftime ceremony.

- Attended eighteen NCAA basketball tournaments.

- Attend the Super Bowl in Phoenix, Arizona.

I feel very blessed to have a successful son, David, who has always taken time from his busy schedule to make sure I could enjoy many activities that I never would have been able to experience otherwise. David, thank you for all your support and input throughout this process. I could never have completed this book without your encouragement. You are the best son a father could have. Your gift of laughter, energy, and fun have always made our family whole. You have made me so proud and I appreciate all you have done for our family. Thank you to Susan and Karen, my accomplished and caring daughters who have always been there for us. Finally, I am especially grateful to have had such a wonderful partner in my wife, Jean, to live this adventure with me.

About the Author

CHARLES L. NOVAK was born in Haddam, Kansas, in 1929. He joined the U.S. Coast and Geodetic Survey as a young man and traveled the United States for much of his life measuring unmapped land. During his time on the road with the USCGS, Charles met his wife, Jean, and they had three children. He retired from the Survey in 1985, but continued work in a position with the U.S. Boundary Commission. He has made his home in more than sixty places across the U.S. and now lives permanently in Scottsdale, Arizona.

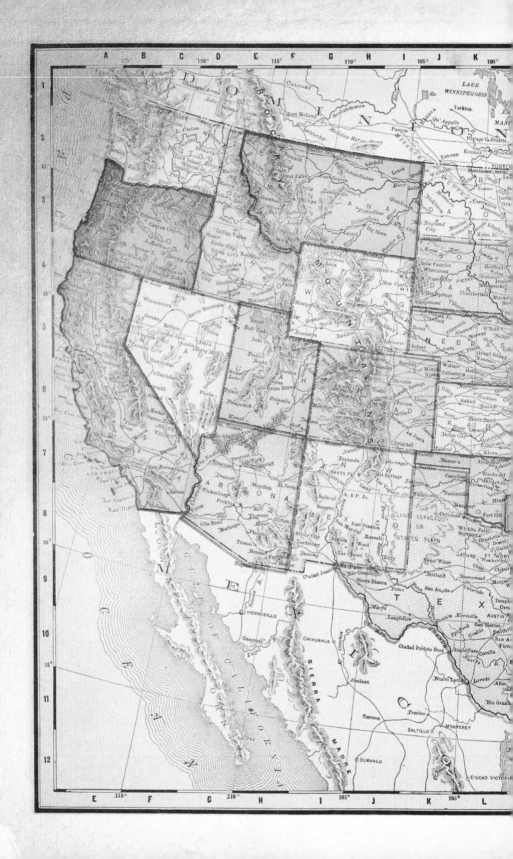